WOMEN'S RIGHTS

WOMEN'S RIGHTS

The
Suffrage Movement
in America,
1848-1920

ॐ

by
Olivia Coolidge

Illustrated with Photographs

E. P. Dutton & Co., Inc.
New York

ॐ

Contents

જી

WOMEN'S RIGHTS

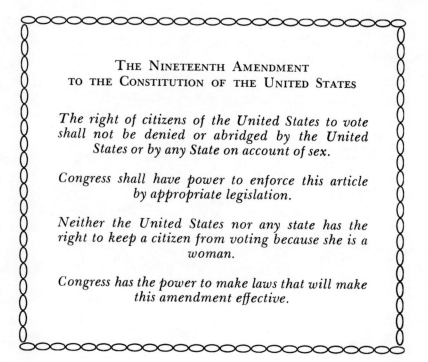

THE NINETEENTH AMENDMENT
TO THE CONSTITUTION OF THE UNITED STATES

The right of citizens of the United States to vote shall not be denied or abridged by the United States or by any State on account of sex.

Congress shall have power to enforce this article by appropriate legislation.

Neither the United States nor any state has the right to keep a citizen from voting because she is a woman.

Congress has the power to make laws that will make this amendment effective.

Introduction

႘

In 1874, the electors of Michigan were asked to decide by state-wide referendum the question of giving suffrage to women. Susan B. Anthony, one of America's most distinguished women, was standing beside a polling booth on election day, asking everybody to vote for the suffrage ticket. A dirty-looking man with a ballot sheet in his hand stopped opposite her.

"What kind of a ticket is that?"

"Why, you can see for yourself," Miss Anthony said, pointing to the place on his paper.

"But I can't read."

"What? Can't you read the ballot you have there in your hand—which you are about to vote?"

"No, I can't read at all."

"Well," explained Miss Anthony, "the ballot means that you are willing to let the women, as well as the men, vote."

He shook his head. "Is that so? Then I don't want it. The women don't know enough to vote."

The man had a point—of a sort. Women's education had lagged behind men's ever since the country was first settled. Even Miss Anthony had no schooling after the age of seventeen. Women's claim to the vote was based not on their learning but on their need. In a man's world, their defenselessness was terribly exploited.

In 1873, a woman in Massachusetts slipped and fell on ice. Being a woman, she was unable to sue for damages. Her husband, however, was awarded thirteen hundred dollars by the courts as compensation for his loss of her labor—money he could spend as he pleased, without consulting his wife. One man who failed in business was supported for years by his wife, who established a successful milliner's shop. Eventually he died, leaving her shop and her savings, legally his own, to somebody else. If he had not made this unjust will, his widow would have received only a third of the real estate. Had he died in debt, everything she had would have been sacrificed to pay off his creditors—although the law did allow her to keep her own clothes, a single table, six chairs, six plates, six knives and forks, one sugar bowl, and twelve spoons.

When a poor woman such as this lost her little business, she found herself, uneducated and unprotected, at the mercy of employers of cheap labor. Mill workers at Lowell, Massachusetts, who were supposed to enjoy model conditions, testified in 1846 while agitating for a ten-hour day that they lived six to a room and two to a bed in company boardinghouses and that their wages after deduction for board were about two dollars a week.

Male gallantry, which was supposed to be at woman's service, did not exist for the poor. Indeed, man's whole claim to be a protector of women was eloquently demolished by Sojourner Truth, an illiterate former slave:

The man over there says women need to be helped into carriages and lifted over ditches, and to have the best place everywhere. Nobody ever helps me into carriages or over puddles, or gives me the best place—and ain't I a woman? Look at my arm! I have plowed and planted and gathered into barns, and no man could head me and ain't I a woman? I could work as much and eat as much as a man—when I could get it—and bear the lash as well! And ain't I a woman?

In every walk of life there were too many women to whom the chivalry of the male gave no protection.

Out of indignation at the condition of women the suffrage movement was born. For seventy years it played a leading part in a great struggle to raise womankind to an equality with men. But by the time suffrage was won, the vote had become more than a symbol—more even than a potent weapon with which women might extort their rights. In the 1870s things had already been changing. Four years before Miss Anthony stood at the polls in Michigan, the state university had been opened to women. Educated women in the modern sense of the word were already beginning to press for general social reforms that had not so far appealed to the men in power. By 1920, when the vote was won, the modern woman was a very different species from her grandmother. She had the ability, the education, the independence to look around her. Somewhat aloof from the commercial and political world, she viewed conditions with a fresh eye. By the time she got the chance to make herself felt in the political world, there were many reforms not primarily for her own good she wanted to make. The women's movement does not end with winning the vote. Indeed, it still goes on, to the benefit of all.

1

The Pioneers
1820–1848

On August 12, 1818, there was a crisis on the Stone farm near West Brookfield, Massachusetts, about twenty miles from Worcester: a thunderstorm threatened to spoil the hay. Farmer Stone and his hired men rushed out to save the crop, leaving Hannah at home alone except for the younger children. She had borne seven already, and there was another coming.

Such farm emergencies were usual. Eventually the men would troop back hot and tired for their evening meal. Meanwhile, Hannah Stone baked bread and cooked dinners over a wood stove in a stifling kitchen on those hot summer days. Her household tasks included the washing up, the laundry, and the scrubbing. She drew water from an outside well, heated it on the stove, and carried it out again to throw it away. She did the canning, churned endless pounds of butter, made cheese or soap, plucked chickens, and dipped candles. She wove and dyed cloth, she cut and sewed the children's clothes.

Hannah's household consisted not only of her husband and children, but also of the hired hands who boarded with them, and her husband's friends. Farmer Stone had three old cronies who were bachelors but liked a comfortable life. One of them was practically always staying at the farm, helping out, no doubt, with the men's chores, but adding to Hannah's. She had no help except from an unmarried sister-in-law who earned her keep as her brother's unpaid servant. On this particular occasion, even Sally does not seem to have been present.

There were eight cows to be milked by hand, which meant pails had to be carried and work done in the dairy as well. All this fell to Hannah because the men had gone out. It had not

occurred to Farmer Stone that it might be more important to
save his wife than to save the hay. Her baby was due at any
moment. But endless babies and endless drudgery were the lot
of women.

That night the baby was born, a girl whom they named Lucy.
Hannah Stone was not a complaining woman; but when she was
told she had a daughter, she exclaimed, "Oh dear! I am sorry it
is a girl. A woman's life is so hard!" In this fashion Lucy Stone
was introduced into a man's world.

She was an obedient child who took readily to chores from
her earliest years. Her older brothers lost no time pointing out
her inferiority. They were favored in the household and accepted the situation as their right. Lucy could not. She noticed,
as they did not, the endless toil and hopeless fatigue of her
mother. Why should her father make every decision and have
the best of everything, Lucy wondered.

She found the answer one day in the Bible. "Thy desire shall
be to thy husband, and he shall rule over thee" the Bible said.
Lucy read the words, appalled. She could not face growing
up to be like her mother, yet the Bible was the book of truth.
She went to Hannah and asked confidentially if there was anything she could take which would kill her.

Hannah Stone tried to console her daughter, but there was
nothing constructive she could say. Every trouble on earth, she
knew, was a result of the apple Eve had given to Adam in the
Garden of Eden. Sin and suffering were woman's fault. She
was the unworthier half of man and must make up for it by hard
work and obedience. The New Testament reinforced the
Old. St. Paul, a bachelor, lived in an age when freedom of
women was fashionable only among wealthy Romans, whose
moral outlook he despised. But Paul's instructions, given in another age and for other reasons, were still binding. None were
more set against any form of advancement for women than the
ministers, particularly those of the Protestant churches.

Lucy seemed to accept her lesson, but inwardly a mind as
stubborn as her father's was at work. It could not be possible

that half of mankind must slave for the other half. The Bible she read was a translation into English done by men. Perhaps they had cheated. Lucy made a great resolve. She was going to college in order to study Hebrew, Latin, and Greek, and find out for herself.

It was a childish ambition. No woman in the whole United States held a college degree. Farmer Stone was the last man to approve such a project, even though he was already disappointed in Lucy because she was not pretty. Tiny, dark, round-faced, with clear gray eyes and high complexion, Lucy appeared younger than her age. Plain she was, but hers was a wholesome plainness which attracted by its sincerity.

She was in her early teens when her father felt she had had enough schooling. Reading, writing, spelling, and figuring were all a woman needed. Lucy was already deep in a plan she had concocted with some of the ambitious students of the town. They would get together and hire a college student to teach them advanced subjects. This naturally would cost money, but the Stones' contribution would be the young man's board. There was always plenty extra to eat on the farm.

Farmer Stone, who had sons to educate, gave in for a brief time. A little later Lucy had a fresh argument ready. At sixteen she would be qualified to teach and thus could earn money. If her father would lend her what it cost to educate her till then, she would pay him back.

Farmer Stone was a prudent, saving man; and it was a pleasing prospect to have a daughter who could earn. But he made her sign a note to repay the money. Lucy Stone was launched at sixteen as a teacher with her board and a dollar a week, out of which, after repaying her father, she proposed to finance a higher education.

It took Lucy nine years to save up seventy-five dollars to enter Oberlin, the only college in the country then offering a degree to women students. It is true that by that time she had enjoyed snatches of education in a couple of private schools and one term at Mount Holyoke, which Mary Lyon had recently founded for the education of young women. And her salary had risen to sixteen dollars a month, unusual riches for a female. Women teachers were generally paid two dollars a week; men got ten for the same work.

At Oberlin Lucy was able to board for a dollar a week, but this proved too expensive. For the first year she ate in her room, keeping her costs down to fifty cents a week. She did housework for three cents an hour and two hours daily of teaching for twelve and a half. During the vacations, she also taught.

Lucy Stone (*From* LUCY STONE, *by Alice Stone Blackwell*)

Her matter-of-fact letters home giving a picture of her life wore down opposition. After two years, her father wrote that when he was making his own way he had had to get up at one or two in the morning. He had never thought a child of his would need to do the same. He would lend her the money she required—at interest, to be sure. She need not earn it.

In 1847, at twenty-nine, Lucy had her college degree. She had not been popular with the Oberlin authorities, who considered her a troublemaker for all her quiet manner. She was older than most of the other students and had made up her inflexible mind on certain issues with which Oberlin officials did not agree.

Chief of these was slavery. Some of the Oberlin teachers were for slavery, some against it. All joined in condemning the extreme antislavery views of William Lloyd Garrison and his Boston paper, *The Liberator;* Lucy was an ardent devotee of both. Her eldest brother, a minister by now, had led the way. Lucy's sympathies for the slave were easily aroused because as a member of a subject group herself she had a fellow-feeling. Her convictions about the injustices done to women had deepened with the years spent earning her living. Lucy's manner was never aggressive, and her time was occupied. But she found several chances to assert her opinions.

She attended a class in rhetoric in the course of which the male students held a weekly debate to which the women listened. Lucy protested to the department head, supported by her best friend, Antoinette Brown—who had the incredible ambition to go to theological school and become a minister. They were given permission to debate each other and drew a large, curious audience. The result was absolute prohibition for the future. Lucy and Antoinette then organized a secret society, which met in the woods with guards posted, and practiced debating. Later, at commencement, each graduating student produced an essay. The men read their own; those of the women were read by the rhetoric teacher. Lucy protested and again stirred up the class. Unless they could read their own essays, the girls would not write them. Eventually the authorities were forced to graduate Lucy and her friends without the essay. Letting them declaim in public was not to be thought of.

Lucy Stone was determined to become a lecturer. She was already a conspicuous person, a female with a college degree. She had met antislavery people of importance who were anxious to use her talents for the cause. And she wished to speak out for women. A lady lecturer was nearly, but not quite, unheard of. In those days, however, there were practically no public entertainments in small towns. Any visiting lecturer could be sure of an audience, though a woman might find half of it drunken rowdies. Besides her indomitable courage and her education, Lucy had another asset, a beautiful speaking voice—not loud, but clear as a bell. She was a natural orator of an insidious sort: gentle, appealing, sincere, and free from rant. She had brought herself unaided to the point where these talents might be used.

While Lucy Stone was teaching for a pittance, Susan Brownell Anthony, a year and a half younger, was doing the same. Susan was a farmer's daughter from upper New York State. Daniel Anthony was of strict Quaker stock and had received a good education, though short of college. He had married outside the Society of Friends, and his bride, another Lucy, had insisted on a last party before she gave up dancing forever. Daniel had attended, sitting on a bench to watch her till four o'clock in the morning. Very soon afterward, she had married him. Not too much later, the Society was noting with disapproval that Lucy Anthony sang lullabies to her children. She gave up singing as she had dancing, but with it she seemed to give up speech. She did her duty and kept her children at arm's length. Perhaps she was as tired as Hannah Stone.

Daniel Anthony was an interesting man who aspired to be something more than a farmer. He started a small textile mill which prospered, sold it, and moved to build a larger one with the aid of a partner who could raise capital. He was also ambitious for his children. The Society of Friends was the only religious group in New England which admitted women on a basis of equality with men. They could speak in meeting and even become elders. Daniel's mother had been one, and he desired education for his girls as well as for his boys. For many years he housed a tutor who conducted a small private school for the Anthonys and others. When his eldest daughter, Guelma, was sixteen, Daniel took her to Philadelphia to place her in a Quaker boarding school that was being started by a young woman, Deborah Moulson. The following year Susan joined her sister there.

Deborah Moulson's school was probably better than most female academies, but not much. Miss Moulson had an interest in science of a general elementary sort. No languages were offered, and of course no art or music. Literature was represented by the Bible and a couple of religious poems. Composition was chiefly taught by letters home full of improving moral sentiments. These were written by the pupils on their slates, corrected by the teacher, then copied out and sent. The chief emphasis, apart from morality, was on handwriting, spelling, and correct punctuation. The training was best suited to a practical mind, which Susan Anthony had, but it failed totally to enlarge her experience. Art and music remained mysteries all her life. Even novels she could seldom read because they overwhelmed her with an excitement she was not used to.

These drawbacks may be forgiven Deborah Moulson, but she had others. She was ill with tuberculosis and emotionally off balance. She avenged herself on life by inflicting spiritual tortures on her best and most sensitive pupil. She exaggerated Susan's small faults, driving her to despair over the state of her soul, and made light of her sincere efforts. Happily, the two-year stay which had been planned was cut short. A depression and his partner's lack of backing ruined Daniel, who had to give up his mill. His daughters went home.

This was all the formal education Susan Anthony was to have. She was now qualified to teach, and even two dollars a week was of help to the family. Daniel struggled hard, but his health and the times were against him. He went bankrupt. His wife's possessions, his by law, were sold to pay his debts—including articles left her by her father and mother. Luckily they had also entrusted money for Lucy to her brother Joshua. He now used it to buy a farm near Rochester, on which the Anthonys settled.

In time the family grew more prosperous again, but for a while they needed every penny. Susan Anthony learned economy in the same hard way Lucy Stone had, but her savings were not her own. Susan was well into her twenties before her abilities made her headmistress of a female academy in Canajoharie, New York. Here she boarded with cousins and found herself earning a hundred and ten dollars a year which she could at last spend on herself.

Canajoharie was a small place, but it had the advantage of being on the Erie Canal. It was linked to the bustling world and gave Susan Anthony new ideas and sophistication. The cousins were congenial and, being on her mother's side, were not Quakers. Susan made herself a plaid dress, bought a shawl, a bonnet, other dresses. People told her she looked nice, and she enjoyed it.

She was rather late for blooming by now. She had had a normal girlhood, but under the influence of Miss Moulson had discouraged beaux. Since then, she had not had opportunities. Harsh-featured, short-sighted, large and clumsy-looking, she had a cast in one eye which embarrassed her greatly. Discovering at twenty that the condition could be corrected by a simple operation, she had it done, only to find that the local expert had done the job badly. Instead of turning inward, the eye now turned slightly outward. At Canajoharie she did not attract men. In truth there was far more to Susan Anthony than had yet appeared. She would have needed a remarkable man and did not meet one.

She liked Canajoharie, but she soon wanted to go home. By 1850 the farm near Rochester was going well, and Daniel was supplementing his income by selling insurance. What was more, he was meeting fascinating people. Rochester was a lively town and, as often happened, Quaker people were in the forefront of liberal reform. Daniel Anthony had long been a crusader for temperance and had carried his devotion to the point of being expelled by the Society. At the lowest ebb of his fortunes, he had been living in what had once been a tavern and had been approached to allow dancing parties in a room built for the purpose. Otherwise, it was pointed out, young people would dance in a tavern that sold liquor. Daniel allowed the parties and permitted his daughters to attend, though never to dance. The Society expelled him, though he continued to attend meeting. In Rochester he found a cause even more congenial to his ardent temperament. Near the Canadian border, the town was an important station on the Underground Railroad, which smuggled slaves into freedom.

Even a hundred years after the Civil War, it is almost impossible to speak of the Anti-Slavery Society in tones that sound fair to everybody. As the South indignantly pointed out, self-righteous northerners might well have concerned themselves with industrial conditions, which were almost equally shocking. But admitting, as one must, that it is always easier to see the speck in the other fellow's eye, we may add that Anti-Slavery rallied behind it a generous and unselfish emotion—the sort of feeling it is good for a nation to have, however expressed.

The people whom Daniel now met were nationally famous. There was, for instance, Frederick Douglass, the remarkable escaped slave turned Anti-Slavery agent. There was William Ellery Channing from Boston, who came to take charge of a church and who knew both Garrison and his friend Wendell Phillips. There was John Brown. Daniel's two sons went out to Kansas, and one of them fought beside John Brown at Osawotamie.

When such fascinating people came for a meal, Susan was all ears. She had taken over a good deal of the housework from her mother and was gradually giving up teaching, there being no longer need for her to earn. In fact, Susan Anthony was looking around for her opportunity, not knowing that it had already knocked at her door but had not found her in. She was thirty, and Lucy Stone had graduated from Oberlin three years earlier.

In 1848, while these two women were reaching the end of their long apprenticeships, Elizabeth Cady Stanton was founding a movement. In age she was very little ahead of the others, but her circumstances had been comparatively easy. Judge Cady, her father, was a successful lawyer in Johnstown, New York. He was not a feminist, but he had five daughters, a situation that is bound to color a man's acts if not his theories. Elizabeth, maybe, was a little spoiled. At Johnstown Academy she had used her position as daughter to the town's most prominent man to edge herself into boys' classes in Greek and higher mathematics. She was trying to make up to her father for the loss of his only son, not perceiving that her academic success embarrassed him.

The Judge's office was in his own house, and Elizabeth liked to sit in a corner during his business hours. She had seen distraught women come in for help and leave in tears. "No, I can do nothing for you. . . . You are entirely in your husband's power. . . . Your earnings are his, and he may spend them as he pleases. . . . You are only entitled to a third of your husband's estate. . . . No court will listen to your complaint, since a woman cannot give evidence. . . . I can do nothing, nothing, nothing." Judge Cady was sorry when he saw that his daughter was upset. He explained gravely that it was his duty to carry out the law, not to change it. Later, however, when she was grown herself, she might petition the New York legislators for improvements.

He did not really suppose she would do so, and nothing was further from his mind than to encourage such a course. He had merely been pointing out that she would have the right of petition. Circumstances, however, caused Elizabeth to remember.

As she grew older and developed a taste for argument, her

father's law pupils liked to put Elizabeth in her place by explaining in legal terms just what her disabilities were. When she married, she would have scarcely any more legal existence than her husband's horse or dog. Her husband could beat her if he cared to. He would own her children, her earnings, even her dress and ornaments. She would be dependent on him during his life, and afterward on her children. If he died intestate, she would get a third of his estate, no more; the rest went to the nearest relative. When he did make a will, he could if he liked leave her nothing. If her father left her money, it must be put into the hands of her husband or possibly of trustees. In any case she would see nothing of it, since the income would be her husband's to spend as he pleased. She could not even dispose of it by will without his consent.

If Elizabeth did not develop the same hard core of resentment as Lucy Stone, it was merely because life was too gay. Petite, blue-eyed, intensely alive, she soon had plenty of admirers. But her intelligence demanded nourishment. She urged her father to give her a chance for higher education.

Elizabeth was always hard to resist. Judge Cady yielded. College was out of the question, but he did send her to Troy Seminary, recently founded by Emma Willard. Troy offered courses in subjects which were advanced for women then, while preserving a domestic, feminine atmosphere.

This was the best Judge Cady would do. When school was over, he expected Elizabeth to come home and get married. He did not imagine there would be any difficulty. Her sister Tryphena had married one of his law students, a very sensible match. It was unthinkable that Elizabeth should lack suitors.

Elizabeth went home and found Johnstown dull. There was a touch of unrecognized genius in her. She was in love with ideas, and would remain so all her life. How could she descend to the level of a chattering crowd of girls bred not to think? Luckily for Elizabeth she had the occasional stimulus of a visit to a cousin.

Gerritt Smith was a prominent liberal of the times. Im-

mensely wealthy and devoted to all sorts of advanced causes,
Smith had made his house a center for reformers, writers, and
thinkers. Among them was youngish Henry B. Stanton, who
was thought of in Gerritt Smith's circle as something of a hero.
He had walked out of Lane Seminary in Cincinnati when Dr.
Lyman Beecher announced that no discussion of slavery would
be permitted. He had done this though he had made great
sacrifices to get there. Since then he had been an agent of the
American Anti-Slavery Society, spreading its views through the
country in a series of lectures. He had been heckled, hustled,
threatened, actually stoned. Churches in which he had spoken
had been set on fire. Henry Stanton, ten years Elizabeth's senior,
now fell in love with her.

Elizabeth was sincerely flattered by the attention of a greater
man than had hitherto come her way. She took him at the
Smiths' valuation and fell in love with the hero, if not exactly
with the individual. He proposed; she accepted.

Judge Cady was horrified. He had the lowest opinion of
abolitionists, was not a liberal, and thought the young man a
silly visionary. Besides, Stanton had no profession and no income. Anti-Slavery paid bare expenses and offered no future.
Judge Cady flatly said it would not do.

Elizabeth gave in to her father for the time. Even Henry
Stanton must have seen that without the Judge's help the marriage was hopeless. But she was unhappier than anyone dreamed.
Johnstown was too small to hold her. She belonged among the
progressive thinkers of her time. She had taken to the atmosphere of the Smiths' circle like a duck to water.

Henry Stanton retired temporarily defeated; he did not give
up. Elizabeth, he felt, was worth persistence. Presently the
Anti-Slavery Society selected him as one of their delegates to
the Anti-Slavery Convention in London, offering a paid trip and
expenses. He rushed to Elizabeth. A trip to London! Why not
marry him and take a chance? The future would look after
itself.

It was a change of atmosphere, a door opening onto the great world. Elizabeth, bored and frustrated, was in a mood to venture. She agreed to get married.

The bridal pair arrived in London in high spirits. Life was a great adventure just beginning. It did not, however, take the shape they had expected. The first event was a violent dispute within the Convention.

Anti-Slavery was to the Americans a domestic issue but a colonial one to the British. In England it involved meetings, propaganda, pressure on Parliament—all male activities. In America, any man who proposed to hide an escaped slave in his barn had better be sure his wife would back him up. Moreover, women—though too little educated to take interest in distant affairs—were capable of seeing evils before their eyes. Women were already entrenched in the American Anti-Slavery Society, and some women delegates had been sent to London. Their British hosts were horrified by their arrival. It was clear that there was going to be a fight before the women were seated.

Trouble started even before the Convention opened. The women's position was ably defended by Mrs. Lucretia Mott, to whom Elizabeth Stanton took an instant fancy. Indeed, Lucretia Mott was one of those rare persons who are universally beloved by those who know them. By religion a Quaker and married to a Quaker, she had escaped the treatment most women received at that time. Cultivated, intelligent, fairly well-to-do, she and her husband had devoted themselves to good works, of which Anti-Slavery was chief. A notable hostess, Mrs. Mott was a true center of all that was best in American liberal thought. Quietly but insistently she had used her prestige to forward the cause of women.

Lucretia Mott's own career had broken precedents. She had become a traveling speaker in Quaker meetinghouses, by merit rather than the result of any set purpose. She had been present with her husband when the Anti-Slavery Society was formed. During the discussion she had risen with modest apologies to clarify a point or two, which she had done so effectively that the astounded men had not objected. A few weeks later she had helped to create a Women's Anti-Slavery Association, one of the first women's groups to be formed in the United States. She was still its president at the time of the London Convention.

Mrs. Mott fought the women's battle in London with considerable persistence and skill. The best she could do, however, was to force the issue onto the floor of the Convention, instead of having the women rejected by the Executive Committee. In the end she lost, even the Americans by no means all supporting her cause. Elizabeth Stanton listened to New England ministers among the delegates opposing the women with the help of quotations from St. Paul. The experience confirmed a distrust of that Apostle and for organized religion that would make difficulties for the movement in the future.

The women were allowed to watch the Convention from the gallery and hear what they could. Highly indignant, Lucretia Mott and Elizabeth Stanton preferred to tour London. Each recognized in the other much to admire. In Lucretia, Elizabeth had found a wise friend. Lucretia had faced all the problems that lay in store for a woman reformer, but had never become discouraged. The situation which had brought the two together broke down the barriers of their difference in age. Both loved to discuss ideas. Elizabeth even laid plans for a meeting of women somewhere to talk over their grievances. She and Lucretia aired views on what should be said.

Henry Stanton spoke so well at the Convention that the English Society asked him to stay on and give a series of lectures. It was nearly a year later that Elizabeth and Henry returned home. Judge Cady had had time to get over his indignation and perceive that he could not, as he had threatened, disinherit his daughter. He would have to do something for Stanton. Henry, for his part, now felt the responsibilities of marriage. He entered the Judge's office to study law.

When he had qualified, he tried to set up practice in Boston, where his Anti-Slavery friends chiefly were. He had enemies there also, however, and work did not flow in. Eventually he moved to Seneca Falls, New York, and established himself there.

Elizabeth felt trapped. Her circumstances were comfortable, but she had children by now. Seneca Falls was small and remote. Interesting people did visit Henry, but her share in their entertainment was housekeeping. She was too busy with her work and her babies to take part in discussions. Besides, she could not conceal it from herself: the men did not want her. Inwardly she fumed. Her affection for Henry was perhaps wearing a little thin. He was not the exceptional person she had thought. In any event, she had not intended to be busied with cooking and diapers while Henry sat in the parlor exchanging ideas.

She had kept up correspondence through the years with Lucretia Mott, and in 1848 she had the exceptional pleasure of seeing her again. The Motts were staying with friends at Waterloo, and Elizabeth could go over for a visit.

She found Lucretia with a few other women, all of Quaker persuasion and liberal habits of thought. To them she poured out her complaints. A stupider woman than Lucretia Mott might have dismissed her as a bad wife and mother, which would have done Elizabeth a great injustice. An excellent housewife and a notable cook, she had already worked out principles of baby care far more advanced than those of her doctors. She was not angry with Henry, or even precisely with fate. She was merely furious with the way in which women were disregarded. Her own troubles served her as a start. Conversation ranged widely over disabilities of all sorts—social, civil, and religious.

Why not do something about it? Encouraged by the ladies present, Elizabeth Stanton was afire with ideas. She would start with a meeting, a woman's convention, in Seneca Falls. What if the town was no great place? The important thing was to make a beginning.

Lucretia Mott agreed. She promised to come back and speak, undertaking that her husband would preside. But an inspirational talk would not start anything. They needed an agreement

which would be there when the meeting was over, one that
could be signed and published.

Casting over possibilities in her mind, Elizabeth thought of
the Declaration of Independence. That was what they wanted!
A Declaration of *Woman's* Independence! Why should not the
original do? They pulled it out and went over it together.
". . . self-evident that all men *and women* are created equal,
that they are endowed . . . with certain inalienable rights. . . ."
With the addition of *women* everywhere and a new statement of
purpose at the end, it would certainly do. Consideration of
practical points, such as money, would have to wait. There was
plenty to start on.

Elizabeth Stanton returned to Seneca Falls in high excitement. She must find a hall and draft an announcement and see
that it got publicity. She must draw up concrete resolutions.
The Declaration's preamble was all very well in itself, but it
was too general to serve as a basis for future action. The meeting
would have to decide what women should fight for.

To draw up a list of demands was easy. Elizabeth's smattering
of legal knowledge helped. There was the right of women to
own property, to own their own earnings, to share in the custody
of their children, to gain education, to enter the professions.
. . . What other rights should she include? Some required
changes in law, others in custom. It was obvious, moreover, that
the list must not be too long. Elizabeth grappled with the complex problem. In the course of doing so, an inspiration came
to her. If women had the vote, they would soon change
the laws—and the customs, too. Yes, the vote was fundamental.
She did not dare adopt it as her sole aim, but she put it on the
list.

Immediately it appeared that her demand for the vote had
raised a tempest. Even dear Lucretia Mott said, "Thou will
make us ridiculous. We must go slowly."

Henry Stanton vowed that if she insisted on votes for women
he would not back her. In fact, he would humiliate her by leaving town on the day of the meeting. But Frederick Douglass, the

Negro abolitionist in Rochester, approved her proposal in his paper *The North Star*. He even promised to speak at the convention. Thus encouraged, Elizabeth stuck to her guns; and Henry did leave town.

In this unpretentious way a movement was launched in Seneca Falls. It was to grow for more than seventy years and end in Tennessee in 1920. Elizabeth Stanton did not see that day, nor did Lucy Stone, or Susan Anthony. Yet of those who have helped their fellow women in America, these three stand first. And of the great crusades for human betterment which have swept this country from that day to this, the suffrage movement has benefited the largest number of persons. Elizabeth Stanton was right: In the course of demanding the vote, women forced remedies for other wrongs.

2

The Fair Beginning
1848–1860

🎜

Charlotte Woodward, one of a farmer's fourteen children, had started to earn her keep at an early age. In addition to their household chores, the women of the family took in work for a local glove-maker. Not a penny of what Charlotte thus earned ever came to her; it all went to her father. At fifteen, she was employed as a teacher in a local school. In 1848 she was seventeen and already established in a boardinghouse near her work. When she heard that a Woman's Rights Convention had been summoned for Seneca Falls, only four miles off, she determined to go. Relations and friends would go with her, and they could borrow the farm cart.

It was a thrilling ride, very likely the longest Charlotte Woodward had ever undertaken. At various crossroads they came in sight of similar carts, all headed for Seneca Falls. There was actually going to be a crowd, perhaps two or three hundred! Charlotte's party arrived in such good time that the place of meeting was still locked. Already, however, people were gathering outside, including about fifty men attracted by the novelty. The women ranged from liberal friends of Elizabeth Stanton to farmers' wives and girls such as Charlotte Woodward.

If men had come to jeer, they were disappointed. Elizabeth Stanton might have an enthusiastic nature, but she had a remarkable head. Her maiden speech was a sound argument, studded with facts. Her Declaration of Independence was received with favor, and the grievances on her list were all approved. Even the demand for the vote, which had shocked Henry Stanton, was carried. There was so much to be said that three days hardly allowed sufficient time.

Charlotte Woodward had plenty to tell her fellow boarders that first evening. Since she was already an abolitionist, Frederick Douglass was one of her heroes. He had been present in person and had actually accepted a ride in the farm cart back to Waterloo, where he was spending the night. To one of her listeners, this was even worse than complaints about the wrongs of women.

"Young ladies who do such things," he remarked icily, "cannot expect attention from gentlemen."

Charlotte gave him a pert answer. A demand had been made and a movement had been started which was to be of importance to her life. A couple of hundred women attended that first meeting, but none of them lived to cast the vote except Charlotte Woodward. In 1920, she was in her ninetieth year. It had been a long wait. "I am going to the polls if they have to carry me," said Charlotte Woodward.

There was so much to be discussed after Seneca Falls that the leaders of the Convention planned a supplementary meeting in Rochester, where Lucy Anthony and her youngest daughter Mary signed the Declaration. Susan, enjoying the comforts of independence in Canajoharie, thought the Convention improper. She was startled by her mother's attending a meeting that had been bitterly attacked by the papers.

Local papers had picked up news of the Convention; and, since the proceedings were novel, New York papers followed suit. With few exceptions, the press was horrified. "This bolt is the most shocking and unnatural incident ever recorded in the history of humanity," began one passage of editorial prose which went on to prophesy that it would "degrade from their high sphere and noble destiny women of all respectable and useful classes, and prove a monstrous injury to all mankind." Ladies taking part in the meetings were represented as unsexed, unnatural creatures and held up to ridicule.

Elizabeth Stanton now found her hands full. Liberal papers were open to her to explain her meeting and her motives. Horace Greeley of the New York *Tribune* was a liberal, and

"Ye May session of ye Woman's Rights Convention. Ye orator of ye day denouncing ye lords of creation." A lively cartoon caricaturing one of the early conventions.
(*The Bettmann Archive*)

his wife was a feminist. He was willing to print correspondence from Elizabeth Stanton. In a smaller way, a ladies' Temperance paper called *The Lily* was being edited in Seneca Falls by a tiny, energetic woman named Amelia Bloomer. Ladies were just beginning to make themselves felt in the Temperance movement; *The Lily* was a new experiment, disarming criticism by its pure title and innocuous contents. Elizabeth Stanton began to contribute excellent articles (signed "Sunflower") on such matters as baby care and household management. This was only a step to airing her opinions on whatever popped into her head, so that *The Lily* began to become a progressive paper, tied to causes only indirectly concerned with Temperance.

While this was going on, Lucy Stone was lecturing for the Anti-Slavery Society. It would not be true to say that no woman had ever given public lectures before, but it was nearly true; and in the smaller towns of Massachusetts Lucy was as novel as a circus. Male opposition was furious and persistent. Lucy learned the hard way that charging a few cents' entrance fee would keep out drunks and rowdies. She tacked up her own notices and every so often used her eloquence on the local boys, who followed behind her tearing them down. Her gentle manner and her Anti-Slavery backing got her a hearing in many a place where the local ministers were against her. Lucy, who always spoke from the heart, found it necessary to justify her appearance on public platforms. The words that rose to her lips formed a general indictment of the wrongs endured by women. In fact, such was her eloquence on this subject that it roused more interest than Anti-Slavery. The Society, which was paying Lucy twenty-five dollars a month, protested.

"I have to speak for the women," Lucy insisted. The men in Boston who formed the nucleus of the Anti-Slavery group were sympathetic. They were liberals infected with the optimism of nineteenth-century reformers. A golden age was coming, and one should miss no opportunity to bring it in. All the same, Anti-Slavery was their real business. A compromise was reached. On weekends Lucy spoke to church audiences on Anti-Slavery. For the rest of the week she defended women. The Society then paid her ten dollars a month. Her little collections covered the cost of halls and the notices printed. Behind her wherever she went she left committees to carry on Anti-Slavery work and woman's rights.

Old systems had broken down. It might have been true at one time that a woman's husband, good or bad, was still her best protector. His worst excesses were restrained more easily by local opinion than by law. But in an industrial era, the opinion of men's neighbors counted for little. Abuse and selfishness were all too common. Besides, women already represented 24 per cent of the industrial total. As wage earners in a man's world, their defenselessness was shamelessly exploited.

Gradually, however, the position of women was rising. Between the time Lucy Stone first thought of going to college and the time she was ready to go, her plan became possible. Elizabeth Blackwell, first woman doctor, graduated from Geneva College in 1849. Through Anti-Slavery or Temperance agitation, a few women had become used to organizing groups for purposes other than sewing or gossip. A proportion of liberal men had faced the fact that a woman might have personality without becoming unfeminine.

These things were working together. Injustices to women were mounting, while at the same time there was a rise in liberal ideas and education. Elizabeth Stanton had founded something that was needed. Other women such as Lucy Stone went to work for other causes and were forced into making women's rights their primary aim. Whatever reform they might have at heart, they could achieve nothing without defending their right to speak at all. Presently liberals in Massachusetts got together and planned a National Woman's Rights Convention in Worcester.

The National Woman's Rights Convention in 1850 was another true landmark of the movement. Well planned in advance and supported by liberal men as well as women, it succeeded in drawing a thousand people from eleven states. To be sure, it was denounced as "a motley gathering of fanatical mongrels, of old grannies, male and female, of fugitive slaves and fugitive lunatics." But Horace Greeley of the New York *Tribune* was present, and speeches were fully reported in his paper. Susan Anthony, reading the speech of Lucy Stone, was converted at last to the woman's cause, which after this convention could call itself a national movement.

When Susan Anthony went home to Rochester from Canajoharie, she soon found herself in demand as a delegate to teachers' conventions. She had experience and natural leadership qualities. She had three hundred dollars saved and was free to travel. Thus, in 1853, she was present with a thousand other women at a teachers' convention in Rochester where the general lack of respect for the teaching profession by the public was long debated. After some hours, Susan Anthony arose to speak.

The president, a professor from West Point, handsome in a

blue coat with brass buttons, caught his thumbs under his armpits and came to the edge of the platform to ask what the lady wanted—"just as if I had fainted or something of the sort," said Miss Anthony. She replied, however, that she wished to speak on the question.

There was a running to and fro while gentlemen on the platform consulted with others on whether a woman delegate had a right to say anything at all. Some said yes, others said no. The president asked the opinion of the meeting. Half an hour of heated debate ensued among the men, while Susan Anthony, quiet, respectable, impeccably neat, stood waiting. Eventually a vote was taken (of the men, of course) and permission was granted. Thereupon Miss Anthony, in a short but trenchant speech, disposed of the question at issue. "Do you not see," she remarked, "that so long as society says a woman is incompetent to be a lawyer, minister, or doctor, but has ample ability to be a teacher, that every man of you who chooses this profession tacitly acknowledges that he has no more brains than a woman?"

Three men came across the floor to congratulate her, while even the Rochester *Democrat* agreed that she had hit the nail on the head. But the female teachers whispered, horrified, "Did you ever see anything like this performance?" "I felt so mortified . . ." "Who can that creature be?"

A similar situation had arisen in the preceding year in the Temperance ranks. Susan had attended a meeting in Albany as a delegate of the Daughters of Temperance and had attempted to speak. Here, however, she was ruled out of order. She walked out, followed by a few friends, found a place for a women's meeting, had a notice inserted in the paper before nightfall, and organized the Woman's State Temperance Society with a convention in Rochester the following spring. The woman's movement was acquiring a leader who could act.

She had thought of herself at first as a Temperance worker, but it had been inevitable that her abilities would bring her into contact with Amelia Bloomer and then with Elizabeth Stanton. In fact, the three ladies had met on the street of Seneca

Falls in 1851 while Susan was staying there with Mrs. Bloomer. She had heard much of Elizabeth by that time and, conscious of her own defective education and provincial background, was prepared to be awed. Elizabeth for her part was attracted by Susan's plain, honest face, her plain, neat dress, and her unself-conscious frankness. A further meeting between them developed a friendship which was to inspire the woman's movement for forty years.

Differences of opinion might arise, but no sign of a quarrel, no shadow of jealousy ever marred their relationship. They met on terms of perfect equality, yet each had her own place. It is significant that Miss Anthony always addressed her friend as "Mrs. Stanton" while answering herself to the name "Susan." Mrs. Stanton, it was understood, must be the leader. She presided while Susan organized. She drafted the great petitions, appeals, and speeches which she or Susan then delivered. Susan did most of the traveling, most of the hard work, provided the facts, and prodded Mrs. Stanton into action. This seemed to her quite fair because she was a spinster with few other demands on her time.

Mrs. Stanton had seven children, the last not born till 1859. With her usual efficiency Elizabeth had discovered a competent housekeeper and made her happy. But she did not subscribe to the notion that children needed only to be well fed and kept out of mischief. She was a mother who gave freely of her time and thought. At intervals "Aunt Susan" would appear with a determined look in her eye, and "Mother" would be closeted with her for a week or a month, as the case might be. If a speech was necessary, frequently Aunt Susan would take full charge while Mother was away. The Stanton children were fond of Aunt Susan, but a little awed by her. There was nothing awesome about Mother, plump and jolly with graying sausage-shaped curls all over her head.

It was natural that the Woman's State Temperance Convention called by Susan Anthony in 1852 should invite Mrs. Stanton to give the chief address and then proceed to elect her president. The Association thereby signed its own death warrant. Temperance, led largely by clergy, could not assimilate Elizabeth Stanton. The churches were opposed to woman's rights, while Elizabeth was outraged by things the Bible said about women. To make matters worse, she had lately shifted her attention to the state of the divorce laws and was proclaiming in her usual forthright way that habitual drunkenness on a husband's part was sufficient cause for dissolving a marriage. Men, who had been allowed in the women's organization as associate members, had a right to speak and soon formed an opposition. The result was a foregone conclusion. Mrs. Stanton was defeated for the presidency in 1853, and Susan Anthony resigned from membership. The Association lingered for a short while without its moving spirit, then dissolved.

This proved the parting of the ways for Susan Anthony, and not without reason. Temperance was not disposed to make a place for women. That very spring there had been a meeting in New York of the Friends of Temperance to plan a World Temperance Convention for the fall. It had been reluctantly conceded that women might be admitted as delegates; but when the further suggestion was made that Susan Anthony should be included on the planning committee, a furor arose. The upshot was that women delegates were barred from the convention altogether. They withdrew, accompanied by some of the men, to form a *"Whole* World's Temperance Convention" of their own. Antoinette Brown, Lucy Stone's college friend, was persuaded to attend the original meetings by promise of fair treatment. As soon as she came forward, however, the proceedings degenerated into a riot. The position of women became the point at issue instead of Temperance itself. Horace Greeley summed up three days of debate in the following words in the *Tribune:*

"This convention has completed three of its four business sessions, and the results may be summed up as follows:

First Day: Crowding a woman off the platform.

Second Day: Gagging her.

Third Day: Voting that she shall stay gagged.

Having thus disposed of the main questions, we presume the incidentals will be finished this morning."

Decidedly the Temperance movement was no place for a woman yet. Elizabeth Stanton had been convinced of it all along, and Susan Anthony now came unwillingly round to her view. If women were to achieve anything in the world, a woman's movement was fundamental.

The fury of the Temperance leaders against their women delegates was really no more than the echo of an outcry in conservative circles against the young feminist movement. That its leaders were unsexed creatures was suspected. Positive proof of this was offered by their support of that most indelicate innovation, dress reform.

Elizabeth Smith Miller, daughter of Gerrit Smith and intimate friend of Elizabeth Stanton, was a lively young woman with money, style, and liberal ideas. She had a real interest in dress and found the mid-nineteenth-century costume with its tightly corseted waist and voluminous petticoats unfitted for either exercise or work. It was uncomfortable and, she was sure, unhealthy. It swept the ground, gathering dirt. It needed at least one hand and considerable skill before it could be gathered high enough to ascend stairs or carriage steps. In fact, it was good only for sitting on sofas. Elizabeth Miller aspired to introduce a more practical style.

It was easy to see that skirts ought to be shorter. Those were days, however, in which the most casual mention of a lady's legs was an indelicate thing. If forced to bring them into conversation, one must politely disguise the fact, saying carefully, for instance, "She broke her *limb*." If legs might not be mentioned, far less could they be seen. No lady feminist dared uncover an ankle.

Elizabeth Miller's solution to the problem of a shorter skirt was a pair of loose Turkish trousers gathered around the ankle and concealing eight inches or so of lower leg. The result was, to say the least, not becoming. The uncorseted waist, wide skirt

Advertisement of the Bloomer costume in *The Lily*, 1852. Tradition states that the two ladies represent Mrs. Stanton (*left*) and Mrs. Bloomer. They bear little resemblance to them as portraits but may well reproduce the details of their individual dresses. (From *The Lily*)

to mid-calf, and baggy trousers beneath gave a tentlike look to the wearer's costume which was accentuated by the wraps and shawls of common outdoor wear. Some women, however, look pretty in anything. Elizabeth Miller was able to carry off her new style. It actually suited tiny Amelia Bloomer. Elizabeth Stanton, whose dumpy shape was not flattered, was entranced by being able to run upstairs with baby in one arm and diapers on the other without tripping over her skirt. Even Lucy Stone was pleased by a practical costume that was at the same time perfectly modest—or so she thought.

The papers at large did not share this opinion. Picking up news of the new style from *The Lily,* the press promptly dubbed it "Bloomer costume" and proceeded to raise a furious outcry against ladies in trousers.

Unpleasant though this sort of publicity was, it had its advantages. Any publicity is apt to be better than none for a new movement, especially when advertising funds are modest. The Bloomer costume made ladies of advanced views conspicuous; it brought them together. It also made their lives a martyrdom. They could not so much as go outdoors without being mobbed. Small boys followed, yelling. Drunks and rowdies congregated. People threw things. Curiosity-seekers gathered to stare. Elizabeth Stanton, with her usual trenchant sense, soon perceived that the Bloomer costume would not do. "It is not wise, Susan," she wrote to Miss Anthony, "to use up so much energy and feeling that way. You can put them to better use."

Mrs. Stanton was perfectly right; and Susan Anthony, though anxious to die for her principles, let herself be convinced. The Bloomer costume, after causing a nationwide scandal for two or three years, was abandoned. It had identified and defined the woman's movement at the price of confirming its opponents in opinions they had possessed anyway. But it had not forwarded the serious aims of its leaders. Bring about the right reforms and, as Elizabeth Stanton had foreseen, the rest would follow.

In principle this was an easy decision, but progress was difficult. Not possessing the vote, women had small influence over male politicians. Money for an organization was hard to come by, since women were dependent on their husbands for cash and had to account to them for every penny. Besides, the vast mass of uneducated women were horrified by their advanced sisters and indifferent to their unfortunate ones. Mrs. Stanton and Miss Anthony, however, made a formidable team. Their homes and connections were in New York State, whose constitution was shortly to come up for review and whose legislature had recently passed a somewhat liberal bill granting certain property rights to unmarried women.

In 1854, therefore, Miss Anthony advanced boldly. At a woman's rights convention in Rochester she launched a petition on the subject of property rights for married women. With the aid of a band of faithful canvassers working under great difficulties and at their own cost, she collected ten thousand signatures. The petition was presented to the legislature as a fitting climax to another woman's convention, held in Albany during the session. The whole affair made quite a stir; and Elizabeth Stanton, who had her own important connections, was invited to speak to the joint judiciary committee. Even the horrified Judge Cady, who was threatening, for neither the first nor last time, to cut his daughter off without a penny, was impressed by her closely reasoned and yet impassioned plea which took in suffrage, jury duty, divorce, and widows' rights as well as the question at issue. But though her triumph showed the legislators that a woman could speak as well as a man, it did little to forward the actual bill, which was not passed.

Undaunted, Susan Anthony started another petition and planned a lecture tour throughout the state. There was in her view no time to be lost, since the memories of legislators are short. She therefore started out on Christmas Day, by herself, furnished with a package of petitions she had printed at her own expense, to canvass every county in the state. She actually covered fifty-four out of sixty, traveling by wagon, rail, or sleigh, and tramping snowy streets on foot through the bitterest winter in New York history. Miss Anthony made her own engagements, collected her own entrance fees, held her own meetings. Not naturally gifted as a speaker, she had composed with Mrs. Stanton's help a fact-studded lecture on the question, which could be delivered in two parts. However, all efforts to learn this by heart were a failure. Without her manuscript, panic would drive the words out of her head. Excellent at managing a meeting, incisive in sticking to the point, she made up for deficiencies in speech-making by earnestness and perhaps also by the sheer novelty of her subject.

Physical hardships were meant, she felt, to be overcome.

First her feet gave agonizing trouble, then the pain settled in her back. She had to sit through one whole journey clinging to the seat in front of her in order to minimize the rattle of the train. She held two meetings, however, and went on to Ogdensburg to spend the night with a cousin. Next morning she had to be helped to dress and, since she insisted on going on, carried out to a sleigh, in which she rode for seventeen miles doubled up with her head on her knees. She held two more meetings, got up at four next morning, and went on by stagecoach and train to Watertown, where in desperation she decided on drastic measures. Sitting in a tin tub, she had the chambermaid pour two buckets of icy water over her. Then she wrapped herself in hot blankets and went to sleep, awakening next morning as good, she asserted, as new. But though she completed her task, she was not done with her backache. It returned the following summer and required an extended period of treatment in Boston, a time she used to make the acquaintance of Anti-Slavery and liberal leaders there.

Susan Anthony's own little savings had long been devoted to good causes. At home with her parents she was always welcome, and when money was needed for printing leaflets or for railway fares, Daniel Anthony was eager to help. His means, however, were small. They sufficed merely to allow Miss Anthony to make a start. The sale of literature and the entrance fees had to be used to repay him, as well as to pay Miss Anthony's expenses. In this winter campaign she collected over two thousand dollars, of which seventy-six were left over for future expenses. That plaid dress she had had made in Canajoharie was still doing duty with others of similar date. Susan was an expert needlewoman and understood all mysteries of invisible mending, replacing a worn breadth with a new piece, or even unpicking a faded dress and sewing up the seams again with the inner side outwards. Ten years after Canajoharie, she had one of her dresses made into a skirt and dyed dark green. Those were the days when a new waist or fresh collar and cuffs refurbished an old costume. Susan Anthony well knew the impor-

tance of a decent appearance. It is notable that the opposition
papers called her spinsterish, sharp-featured, plain, or aggressive. One of them even went so far as to say on one occasion
"Susan was quite drunk," while several represented her as smok-
ing large cigars. But neither prejudice nor caricature even suggested she was shabby.

The result of her tremendous single-handed campaign may
be summed up by the report of a committee of the New York
legislature on woman's rights in 1855:

"The bachelors on the committee, with becoming diffidence,
have left the subject pretty much to the married gentlemen.
They have considered it with the aid of the light they have before them and the experience married life has given them. Thus
aided, they are enabled to state that the ladies always have
the best place and choicest tidbit at the table. They always
have the best seat in the cars, carriages, and sleighs; the warm-
est place in winter and the coolest place in summer. They have
their choice on which side of the bed they will lie, front or back.
A lady's dress costs three times as much as that of a gentleman;
and, at the present time, with the prevailing fashion, one lady
occupies three times as much space in the world as a gentleman.

"It has thus appeared to the married gentlemen of your
Committee, being a majority (the bachelors being silent for the
reason mentioned and also probably for the further reason that
they are still suitors for the favor of the gentler sex), that, if
there is any inequity or oppression in the case, the gentlemen
are the sufferers. They, however, have presented no petition for
redress; having, doubtless, made up their minds to yield to an
inevitable destiny."

Funny? No doubt, yet the miseries of married woman were
not imaginary. Everyone knew instances of them, though many
were blind to the tyrannies of everyday life. Susan Anthony,
more sensitive, saw plenty of these. Unable because of drifting
snow to keep an engagement, she took refuge in a little tavern,
"where the landlady was not yet twenty and had a baby fifteen
months old. Her supper dishes were not washed and her baby

was crying, but she was equal to the occasion. She rocked the little thing to sleep, washed the dishes, and got our supper. . . . She gave us her warm bedroom to sleep in, and on a row of pegs hung the loveliest embroidered petticoats and baby clothes, all the work of that young woman's fingers, while on a rack was her ironing perfectly done, wrought undersleeves, baby dresses, embroidered underwear, etc. She prepared a six-o'clock breakfast for us. . . . Now for the moral of this story. When we came to pay our bill, the dolt of a husband took the money and put it in his pocket. He had not lifted a hand to lighten that woman's burdens, but had sat and talked with the men in the barroom, not even caring for the baby, yet the law gives him a right to every dollar she earns, and when she needs two cents to buy a darning needle, she has to ask him and explain what she wants it for."

The mockery of the legislators after all her efforts was discouraging. Another blow at this time of exhaustion put Susan Anthony quite out of patience.

The work of Lucy Stone had been steadily progressing. She had been among the planners of the Worcester Convention of 1850. Through her energies yearly petitions were presented to the Massachusetts legislature. Her presence and eloquence inspired important meetings. Susan Anthony, though never wavering in her loyalty to Mrs. Stanton, had felt herself drawn to Lucy, who never needed to be prodded into work. Lucy, Antoinette Brown, and herself, exulted Miss Anthony, were the work horses of the movement. All of them were spinsters with no family demands upon their time.

This being her view, her dismay may be imagined when 1855 brought the marriage of Lucy to Henry Blackwell and of Antoinette to his brother Samuel. What did it matter that the Blackwell brothers were members of a remarkable family and that Elizabeth Blackwell, pioneer woman doctor, was their older sister? No matter how ardent the Blackwells might be in defense of woman's rights, marriage to them still meant conflicting ties. Plain, blunt Susan, who had herself just refused a decent proposal, could not summon up the strength to be gracious to Lucy. She had just involved herself in a series of meetings which seemed beyond her own unaided strength. Her chief helper had been called home by illness in the family. Her married friends were busy, one and all. It cannot have added to her good humor to receive from the absent Lucy a jocular piece of advice—to get herself a good husband.

Lucy herself had been aware of the conflict between marriage and the cause and had long resisted her suitor. She was thirty-seven and was settling down into the unmarried state. Nor was it in her to forsake the cause for which she had battled from childhood.

That would not be necessary, Henry explained. He was as anxious as she to devote himself to good works and perfectly ready to take up a cause beloved of his wife and sisters. He looked on himself as setting Lucy free to work by assuming the burden of her support.

Lucy was tempted by this view, and Henry's personality was attracitve. Small but well formed, with blue eyes and dark, curly hair and beard, Henry was gentle in manner and yet high-spirited. His humor was a disarming experience for serious Lucy, who had never from childhood ventured a joke. His view of marriage as a partnership exactly matched her own. Between them they drew up a protest against the subjection of women as it was expressed in the marriage service. This they caused to be read aloud before the ceremony. To this bombshell, which was thought by some to deny the validity of the marriage oath, Lucy added another. She wished to be called Mrs. Stone, not Mrs. Blackwell.

These concessions were all very well, but the effect of the marriage was precisely what Susan Anthony had foreseen. Henry had good business abilities but little capital. He embarked on various ventures which involved Lucy and himself in several moves. They soon had a daughter. Lucy was too devoted a mother to leave her child with the Blackwell aunts until she was old enough to bear separation without pain. In fact, though she was always ready to help and was influential in her immediate neighborhood, Lucy Stone abdicated her leadership of the movement—at least for some years. As for Antoinette Brown, considerably younger than Lucy, she had six children in quick succession. Susan Anthony was left to do the heavy work single-handed.

Luckily for Miss Anthony, there were compensations in succeeding to Lucy's position with the liberals in Boston. She was soon elected to the national committee of the Anti-Slavery Society and employed as an agent in the field for ten dollars a week and expenses. Diffident about her lack of education and not naturally eloquent, Susan had hitherto depended on Mrs. Stanton to write her speeches. Slavery, however, had become too emotional an issue for prepared argument. Susan may have ranted, but the daily practice taught her to throw away her notes. It was a valuable lesson.

In return for her work, the interest and support of Anti-Slavery leaders for the woman's movement were forthcoming in an increasing degree. Money, too, came trickling in. A Hovey Fund of five thousand dollars was entrusted to Susan Anthony, Lucy Stone, and Wendell Phillips for the woman's crusade. The Jackson Fund, more magnificent still, gave twenty-five thousand to the same trustees to be spent for the purposes of Anti-Slavery and Woman's Rights in equal proportions.

As things went on in this fashion, the national viewpoint was evidently changing. To be sure, conservatives were irreconcilable. In 1856, Miss Anthony chaired a committee on · co-education and delivered its report. The president of the teachers' association replied: "As much as I am compelled to admire your rhetoric and logic, the matter and manner of your address and its delivery, I would rather follow a daughter of mine to the grave, than to have her deliver such an address before such an assembly."

Strong words, but they concealed a remarkable fact. Three years before, Miss Anthony's little speech at an educational meeting had been allowed only after male debate. Now she sat on committees and delivered reports. Editorials still jeered: "What do the leaders of the women's rights conventions want? They want to vote and hustle with the rowdies at the polls. They want to be members of Congress and in the heat of debate subject themselves to coarse jests and indecent language." Yet in the same papers women's actual speeches were considered news and fully reported. An increasing proportion of the populace read them with approval.

Nowhere was the change in atmosphere more evident than in the New York legislature, on which Miss Anthony's yearly pressure had never relaxed. In 1860, a bill was introduced to provide women with the right to sue in court and to collect their own wages. It also gave widows the same rights as widowers to inheritance and guardianship of children. Elizabeth Stanton, testifying before both houses, spoke for two hours to great effect; and the bill was passed.

It was only twelve years since Elizabeth's little meeting at Seneca Falls, but a revolution in opinion had taken place. Woman's right to appear in public might be deplored, but it was no longer disputed. Her abilities might seem unwomanly, but they were recognized. Her need for legal protection was being met. As Anti-Slavery gained ground in the North, it warmed sympathies for another deprived group, especially as the leadership in both associations was the same. Southerners, meanwhile, called for protection of women in industry as a means of embarrassing the industrial North. Looking backward at how much had been achieved and with what tiny resources, women's leaders were deluded into thinking the rest would be easy. They had set the snowball rolling. At this rate of growth, they thought, in another twelve years they might have the vote!

3

The Split
1866–1869

By 1866, Lucy Stone had put on weight and looked her age. Her broad, red face was framed by hair parted in the middle and scraped into a bun behind. She appeared to be, in fact, just what she was, a middle-aged farmer's daughter, skilled in baking pies and putting up preserves. Her manner was as quietly determined as ever, but domestic life had brought about an inward change. Lucy, the lady lecturer who had faced ribald audiences without a tremor, had lost her nerve. But she was determined to overcome this weakness. The Civil War was now over, and agitation for woman's rights ought to be resumed. Little Alice was old enough to visit her aunts. Besides, her husband, Henry Blackwell, who had retired from business, was now always at her side. Next to the dumpy figure of Lucy, Henry looked smaller than ever. But the twinkle was still in his eye and the bushy whiskers were only touched with gray. Henry shaved his upper lip; and it might be noticed that this was unusually long, while his firm mouth was narrow. This gave his face a strange expression which suggested that his easy manners were not a clue to his whole character. Henry, like Lucy, knew how to hold on tight.

As this formidable pair advanced into the limelight, the woman's movement was facing both opportunity and crisis. None of its leaders had made a great name during the Civil War. Their life work had merely been interrupted by it. But Clara Barton had shown the nation what a woman could do. Anna Dickinson had gained applause from coast to coast as a lady orator. Julia Ward Howe was coming into prominence. Julia's large family of children, her social connections, personal charm,

and distinguished husband were sufficient proof that a womanly
woman could also become a public figure. Behind these outstanding women were thousands of others who had organized to
help the Sanitary Commission in time of war. They were unwilling to retire to domestic life. Meanwhile, the industrial expansion of war had sent increasing numbers into the factories;
the wage-earning women in some towns outnumbered the wage-
earning men.

At the outbreak of war, Anti-Slavery leaders had in effect said
to the woman's group, "Stop agitation. This is no moment to
divide a nation already facing division. Work with us for outright abolition. When we win, we may press your claims, as you
press ours now. There will be a wave of generous feeling, on
the crest of which the woman's movement will ride."

An agreement of this sort was perfectly natural, since the
leaders of each movement were deeply committed to the other.
Susan Anthony and Elizabeth Stanton agreed, but the price of
dropping agitation had been high. In 1862, the New York
legislature withdrew most of the benefits of the great act of 1860.
Relaxation of pressure there had led immediately to a reaction.
Undaunted, however, the two ladies planned a Woman's
Loyal League, which was to produce a monster petition asking
for outright, not conditional, abolition. They desired a million
signatures. Susan Anthony started out to get them on a salary
of twelve dollars a week from the Hovey Fund and with a New
York office bare of furniture except for two borrowed chairs.
Luckily Henry Stanton had moved his family to New York, so
that Mrs. Stanton could offer her friend board at a cheap rate.
Susan lunched on five cents' worth of strawberries (in season),
two tea rusks, and a glass of milk. Having no allowance
for transport, she tramped New York. She scraped up the money
for office rent, postage, printing, and secretarial help by lectures
or appeals to well-wishers. She even charged a penny for signing
the petition and raised three thousand dollars by this laborious
means. Though she did not get her million signatures, she got
four hundred thousand. The work brought her into corre-

spondence with women all over the northern states and greatly
enlarged her vision. It was also an effective contribution to
Anti-Slavery agitation. Quite naturally as the war drew to its
close she looked to the Anti-Slavery leaders—Henry Tilton,
Henry Ward Beecher, Wendell Phillips, and the rest—for her
reward.

The Anti-Slavery leaders, having got abolition, were demanding Negro franchise, without which they foresaw that
illiterate Negroes would be at the mercy of the white South.
The woman's organization, starting into fresh life, held a convention and changed itself into the Equal Rights Association,
devoted to pressing for votes for women and Negroes at the
same time. It had been agreed that the Anti-Slavery Society
should do the same. Mysteriously, however, Wendell Phillips,
now its moving spirit, held off. What was the matter?

The matter was that the Anti-Slavery leaders perceived that
the tide did not run so strongly as they had expected. There was
opposition to Negro suffrage even in the North. It could, they
thought, be won, but not if another unpopular cause were
tacked onto it. They were reduced to imploring the women to
wait a while. "It is the Negro's hour."

This then was Susan Anthony's reward. The Negro's hour!
Woman suffrage, the fundamental issue of the whole woman's
movement, was coming up for the first time; and she was asked
to drop it. She was and always had been an abolitionist. But
she also felt it was not fair that Negroes, illiterate for the most
part, should vote in preference to the most cultured women of
the nation. In fact, she refused to admit that half a good measure was better than nothing at all. She was not prepared to
compromise on this point whereas Lucy Stone, now renewing
connections with her Boston friends, reluctantly was.

In 1867, however, an opportunity arose too tempting for even
Lucy to ignore. The state of Kansas put up two constitutional
amendments, providing for Negro and for woman suffrage. Former Governor Robinson, a prominent Republican politician,
was the brother of Lucy's sister-in-law. He invited the women to

campaign, promising Republican support. Susan Anthony, who had a brother in Kansas, was eager for the fray; and Lucy could not hang back. Overcoming her nervousness, she promised that she and Henry would campaign in the spring if Susan and Mrs. Stanton would follow in the fall before the election.

Lucy did campaign in the spring, and things went well. She regained confidence. Henry had his first experience of speaking for the cause and liked it. Governor Robinson was generous with hospitality and transport. Lucy and Susan, outvoting Wendell Phillips, had forced him to supply money from the Hovey Fund for printing literature. The expense of travel, in the modest circumstances, was not beyond Henry's power to pay. The Stone-Blackwell team came back encouraged. Campaigning in Kansas under frontier conditions had certainly been a challenge. Springless wagons, muddy bottoms, primitive ferries, log schoolhouses, stores with planks on kegs for seats had called for resilience and stamina. Food in the backwoods consisted of dried fish or greasy bacon, sorghum for sugar, milkless coffee, crackers. Bedbugs were everywhere. But with victory manifestly in sight, the experience was worth it.

The campaign of Miss Anthony and Mrs. Stanton opened less prosperously. Wendell Phillips sourly informed them that the Hovey Fund was all spent. As for the Jackson Fund, he had his hand on that and did not intend it to be spent for woman suffrage. Miss Anthony had to raise money for printing and railway fares. Nor, when the ladies arrived, did the prospect look encouraging. The Democratic party had been temporarily wiped out by the war, but the victorious Republicans had split. Former Governor Robinson, it was becoming clear, was on the losing side. The Republican machine was far from ready to support a measure which had been represented as a Republican one. To make matters worse, precisely as the Anti-Slavery leaders had predicted, the two amendments were injuring each other. It began to look as though neither would be adopted.

Thus desperate for funds and resentful of the position into which they had been inveigled, the ladies saw their golden

chance slipping away. Temptation presented itself in the form
of an offer from George Francis Train, Democrat, millionaire,
and Copperhead, to share their campaign. Betrayed by every
ally, including Phillips for whom she had done so much, Miss
Anthony was in a mood to accept help from the devil complete
with horns and tail. The exuberant indiscretion of Mrs. Stanton
was as remarkable as her excellent mind. They accepted the
offer.

George Train, speculator and financier, was a colorful character, personable, very much of a dandy, with a ready tongue,
a number of eccentric interests, and no discretion. As an opponent of "sound money" he was anathema to the financial
magnates of the North. As a Copperhead, he was equally re-
pugnant to Anti-Slavery leaders. He was also a supporter of
Irish independence, the eight-hour working day, woman suffrage, and Train for President. But he was a good speaker and
traveling companion. He had expected the easy assignments and
large audiences, but in the peculiar partnership of the two
ladies, such of these as existed were reserved for Mrs. Stanton.
Although disappointed, Train was ready to prove to Susan
Anthony that he was able to endure primitive discomforts as
well as she. In fact, his attendance lightened her labors, and his
money smoothed her way. Any doubts Miss Anthony might have
had were set at rest by a typical gesture.

"You ought to have a woman's paper," he said to her one day
as they traveled together.

Susan Anthony must have sighed from the heart. It was her
dearest wish. A paper! She could see no other way to bring the
woman's movement into American homes. Yet women could
not pay much. Men would not advertise in a woman's paper.
Even the *Lily* had given up long ago. The *Una,* a later effort,
had never prospered. The woman's movement had no money
of its own to back a paper. It was useless even to discuss it.

Train said nothing more at the time, but in that evening's
meeting he calmly announced that Miss Anthony would launch
a weekly paper to be called the *Revolution,* price two dollars

and motto "Men their rights and nothing more; women their rights and nothing less." Elizabeth Stanton and Susan Anthony heard him in a daze. They had found a backer!

Meanwhile, Lucy Stone scanned the newspaper reports of the Kansas campaign with growing indignation. She might compromise with Wendell Phillips, perhaps, but never with a Democrat like George Train! "Susan Anthony can be scarcely less crazy than he is," she exploded. Her fury was shortly increased. Train was paying expenses of a lecture tour through the major towns of the Midwest. Here, on the same platform as Miss Anthony and Mrs. Stanton, he announced to enormous audiences "Train for President." The outraged Lucy put a notice in the papers that Mrs. Stanton and Miss Anthony were *not* at present touring under the auspices of the Equal Rights Association. She prepared herself to call them to account for misuse of the Association's funds.

To Susan Anthony, after snatching all these triumphs from the failure of the Kansas campaign, Lucy's criticisms came like icy water. In particular, she prided herself on being meticulously honest in financial matters. It was hardly for Lucy, whose own campaign had been quite generously assisted, to criticize one who had raised all the money herself.

"Raised in the name of the Equal Rights Association," pointed out Lucy. "Mrs. Stanton and Miss Anthony have no business to decide how such money is spent."

Miss Anthony, who had had to give Train an answer of yes or no without opportunity to consult her central committee, lost her temper. She felt she had a right to use her judgment. And had she not gained the vital *Revolution?*

"I *am* the Equal Rights Association," she flashed. "Not a soul of you amounts to shucks except myself."

The quarrel was hushed up, but the *Revolution* opened under private auspices, while the rift between Lucy and Susan Anthony continued to widen. Neither of the ladies was petty enough to quarrel solely for personal reasons, yet a difference in principle was certainly hardened by resentment. Susan's attitude to Lucy's marriage had given offense. Thereafter, when Lucy retired into private life, Susan had harried her as she had Mrs. Stanton. Lucy, who required no urging to do her best, was annoyed. Now that she was able to come forward again, she had no intention of being bullied by the two formidable ladies who had for years been the life and soul of the movement.

Matters came to a head at the Equal Rights Convention of 1869. Although the amalgamation between Anti-Slavery and Equal Rights had not taken place, the individual leaders of each of the movements were prominent in the other. Frederick Douglass, earliest supporter of Elizabeth Stanton, was outraged by her association with Train. He bitterly denounced it and, assisted by other men present who were also Anti-Slavery agents, rammed through a resolution committing the Equal Rights Association to support of the Fifteenth Amendment, providing for Negro suffrage. Thus the woman's movement was placed in the position of backing a suffrage amendment excluding women.

This denial of principle was too much for Susan Anthony. Besides, she perceived her dismay was echoed widely among women attending the meeting. Hastily she summoned a group of malcontents to form a new organization, the National Woman Suffrage Association, to work specifically for that end and no other. It was a master stroke. The woman's movement, now sharply defined as a suffrage movement, was separated once and for all from Anti-Slavery. It had thus gained unity and drive, if at great sacrifice. Nobody in it amounted "to shucks" but Susan Anthony—and of course Elizabeth Stanton.

Looking back over the years, one may say that Susan Anthony had performed a notable service to the movement. A high cost, however, was still to be paid. Lucy Stone, who had not been invited to the meeting which had formed the National Association, was bitterly resentful. The Equal Rights Association had voted a measure by a majority of those present. Lucy thought it treachery for a splinter group to hold a secret meeting and try to wrest control of the woman's movement from its elected heads.

The Equal Rights Association was dead. Even Lucy Stone could see that the women in it would inevitably drift toward Miss Anthony unless a rival party were formed to work for woman's rights. That there ought to be such a rival party she was convinced. She did not trust Miss Anthony's good sense and disliked her methods. She hated her partnership with Train and despised the articles he published in the *Revolution*. Lucy was well aware that time and patience might serve to found a woman's party which would be larger and more solid than the National Association Miss Anthony had hastily put together. Thus, under Lucy's prudent management, the American Woman's Suffrage Association soon gathered in a majority of the personnel of the old Equal Rights.

Even more important than Lucy's rival association was its own paper. The *Woman's Journal,* supported by Boston money, had far more reliable backing than the *Revolution.* By 1869, the woman's movement, split into two parts, had missed its chance for an amendment, but was starting again with new independence and clarity of aim. Both organizations had become in name and purpose woman suffrage parties.

4

Susan B. Anthony,
the Invincible
1870–1890

૭

The foundation of the *Woman's Journal* proved a death-blow to the *Revolution*. The feminist movement was too small for two papers, and the more conservative one had wider appeal. Furthermore, Train's enthusiasm soon flagged. At first he used the *Revolution* to publicize his crackpot financial theories (to the indignation of the Stone-Blackwell faction, who objected to these being pinned onto woman's rights). Next he had sailed for Ireland to do great deeds for the nationalists there, leaving six hundred dollars behind him for current expenses. The English government, however, had no use for Irish agitators. Train was held under open arrest in Dublin for nearly a year. Under this emotional strain, he soon lost interest in the fortunes of the *Revolution*. No more money was forthcoming. Susan Anthony had to raise cash herself and was increasingly absent on lecture tours that never earned sufficient funds.

Despite these difficulties, the *Revolution* lived more than two years and, thanks to the abilities of Susan Anthony and the talents of Elizabeth Stanton, was always a lively and well-written paper. It is fashionable nowadays to regret its demise, pointing out a number of respects in which it was superior to the *Journal*. The *Revolution*, vigorously radical, was the first to make an effort to bring working women and immigrants into the movement. Its sympathies were broad, and it was not afraid of taking up issues. The *Journal*, adopting the view that suffrage was its sole object, was afraid to discuss divorce laws, challenge the church, or indulge in the private crusades which appealed to the generous heart of the *Revolution*. A single example may illustrate the difference.

Albert D. Richardson, a reporter on the *Tribune* staff, was openly shot down in the paper's office by Daniel McFarland for being his divorced wife's lover. The fact was that McFarland's brutality and dissolute habits had made the poor woman's life a misery. Richardson had helped her to escape, and she now planned to marry him. Indeed, she did marry him on his death-bed. The press, however, raised a great storm against her. In any marital dispute, the woman must be wrong. Could it be wondered at if a forsaken husband avenged himself in a mo-ment of distraction? After a sensational trial, McFarland was acquitted on the grounds of insanity and, adding injury to in-sult, awarded the custody of their twelve-year-old boy. While Miss Anthony arranged a mass meeting of protest, the *Woman's Journal* refrained from comment. Since none of the parties concerned cared about woman suffrage, the *Journal* did not consider the case its business.

This prudent attitude of Lucy Stone's may seem ungenerous, yet it made tactical sense. Those who lament the passing of the *Revolution* are apt to forget that the *Journal* was better fitted to perform a vital service. If the movement was ever to take on mass proportions, it must not scare away the middle-class woman. The *Journal* was timid, but it was read for that very reason. The services of Lucy Stone to her cause should not be undervalued.

Lucy Stone henceforward chiefly managed the *Journal* and the American suffrage group, always preferring to give othrs the limelight, but reserving to herself power earned by doing the hard work. Mrs. Stanton and Miss Anthony, meanwhile, advancing from one blaze of publicity to another, sought to rouse the country's conscience by a strange alliance and a dra-matic crusade.

In 1871, about a year after the death of the *Revolution,* a handsome young woman named Victoria Woodhull obtained permission to present a petition to the judiciary committee of the House of Representatives in Washington, claiming that the recent amendments to secure the Negro vote had confirmed it to women also. The point was a nice one. The Fourteenth and

Victoria Woodhull addressing the House Judiciary Committee.
(*The Bettmann Archive*)

Fifteenth amendments are careful not to confer the franchise on the Negro. On the contrary, assuming the vote to be a citizen's right, they merely insure that it shall not be restricted by color. But if the citizen has such a right, are not women also citizens? Miss Anthony and Mrs. Stanton were preparing to take up this issue when they discovered that Mrs. Woodhull had got in before them. They attended the hearing and were impressed by Mrs. Woodhull's eloquence. They hailed her as a recruit from a new quarter.

She had been born Victoria Claflin and had, with her sister Tennessee, started out in Ohio as a spiritualist and healer. In Pittsburgh the pair had treated Cornelius Vanderbilt, who presently set them up in a New York brokerage business and gave them tips enough to make them a fair fortune. This in itself created scandal, which was increased by Victoria's marital affairs. Divorcing Woodhull, she married a Colonel Blood, while still allowing Woodhull to make his home in her house. Rumor had it that she needed him to correct her grammar in the spiritualist newspaper she and her sister had established. In any event, *Woodhull and Claflin's Weekly* openly advocated free love, which was too advanced a doctrine even for Mrs. Stanton.

Notwithstanding this difference of opinion, Mrs. Stanton impulsively took up Victoria Woodhull, and Susan followed. To the horror of the *Journal* and the American Association, Victoria appeared on the National's platform. The press, confirmed in its opinion that advanced women would stop at nothing, raked up Mrs. Woodhull's past, attributing her views to the whole movement. It is indeed difficult to defend Mrs. Stanton and Miss Anthony for bringing her forward. It may be remembered, however, that Mrs. Stanton was always impulsive, while Mrs. Woodhull was a notorious charmer. Besides, the two leaders of the suffrage radical wing were hard pressed by the better-organized American Association. Lucy Stone had gathered in the larger section of the movement, adding to it some distinguished new figures, such as Julia Ward Howe. Mrs. Woodhull was a sign of the National Association's desire to look around likewise for fresh support.

Victoria Woodhull's designs were large and ambitious. She had her own following among spiritualists and eccentrics, with whom she attempted to pack the convention of the National Association. A motion to transform the National into a political party was foiled only by the determination of Miss Anthony, who firmly ruled the proposal out of order. She then declared the meeting closed and had the lights turned out, lest a remainder pass inconvenient votes when she had left. The result was that Mrs. Woodhull and her followers held a separate meeting in which she formed her own party, nominated herself for president, and chose for vice-president the Negro Frederick Douglass without asking his consent.

This ludicrous uproar put an end to the association between the National Association and Victoria Woodhull. The newspaper sensation, however, was only beginning. It was already known to a few people that the wife of Theodore Tilton had been having an affair with Henry Ward Beecher, the popular preacher. Mrs. Tilton had confessed the liaison to her husband

and various other persons, including Susan Anthony. The matter concerned the suffrage groups very closely, since Beecher was a former president of the American, while Tilton, editor of a liberal paper, was associated with the ladies of the National. No doubt for this reason, Miss Anthony had confided her knowledge to Elizabeth Stanton. She in turn had indiscreetly passed it on to Victoria Woodhull, who now took her revenge by revealing it in *Woodhull and Claflin's Weekly*.

The fat was at once in the fire. Henry Ward Beecher denied the affair. Tilton, egged on to defend his wife's veracity, brought suit. The scandal became a national sensation. In Beecher's favor were his sacred calling, his immense reputation, and the vested interests of his publishers or pew holders in his innocence. Against Beecher was most of the evidence, on which his supporters tried to throw discredit by vicious attacks on Mrs. Tilton. Mrs. Stanton and the faithful Susan leaped chivalrously to her defense. The publicity, whichever side the papers took, blackened the feminist movement. The American Association was compromised by its close association with Beecher, while the National Association was connected with Victoria Woodhull and Mrs. Tilton.

The Beecher-Tilton scandal burst on the public in November 1872, even as Miss Anthony was making a fresh effort to gain the vote. The congressional committee had as a matter of course rejected Victoria Woodhull's petition, but the logic of it had been for some time apparent. Miss Anthony had spoken widely on the subject, and various petitions from women were now before the courts. She determined to dramatize the issue by voting in the election of 1872.

On the next-to-last day of voter registration, Miss Anthony, accompanied by her sister and a group of friends, descended on a shoemaker's shop in Rochester's eighth ward, occupied by the registrars. These proved no match for her personality. Afraid of the penalties threatened in the Fourteenth Amendment, aware that there was now no time for public discussion, and no doubt reflecting that mere registration was not a vote, they entered the ladies on their lists. Returning on election day, Miss Anthony succeeded in casting her vote, followed by fifteen other ladies who swam in her wake.

As soon as this news hit the papers, the Republican government found itself gravely embarrassed. Grant's first term as President had not been a success. Opposition within the Republican party had been strong enough to nominate Horace Greeley for the office. Greeley, to be sure, had proved too much of an amateur to compete with Grant. Nevertheless, there was no doubt in the government's mind that the second term would not be plain sailing. Reconstruction was still in a chaotic stage, while regional problems of many kinds swelled discontent. The Republicans, in fact, had no intention of adding to their load by adopting a controversial measure such as woman suffrage. Miss Anthony's action, however, had forced them into taking some stand. To do nothing must be construed by everyone as approval.

On Thanksgiving Day, therefore, the United States Chief Marshal, dressed for the occasion in top hat and kid gloves, rang the Anthonys' doorbell and produced warrants. His intention had apparently been to warn the ladies that they were to be arraigned for voting illegally. He may even have chosen the holiday to make his procedure quietly informal. If so, he did not know Miss Anthony well. She refused to answer the summons. If the marshal wanted her to go to court, he would have to take her. The wretched man was forced to round up the ladies and escort them to the courthouse that very day. Naturally the district attorney did not appear, allowing the ladies to complain that they had been left waiting in a grimy little anteroom all day. Next morning, however, in a crowded courtroom, the authorities focused on the ringleader. Miss Anthony was committed for trial and bail was demanded. Somewhat to her indignation, this had to be paid, since she had engagements in the lecture field and a woman's rights convention of the National Suffrage Association just after Christmas.

The trial was set for early May. Susan Anthony, meanwhile,

was the heroine of the hour, both at the National's convention and at the twenty-fifth celebration of Seneca Falls. But none of those who sang her praises offered help. The National Association, although solidly behind its leader, was largely unorganized. It consisted of individuals rather than groups, and was accustomed to leaving difficulties to Miss Anthony. She, therefore, unsupported by her friends, without financial resources, and crippled by debts left by the *Revolution,* was allowed to face the wrath of a government determined to convict her.

Miss Anthony's defense was that the Fourteenth Amendment confirmed her in a right which had always existed. But if this contention was disallowed, she had still voted according to conviction and based on an interpretation of the law which had not yet been dismissed by the courts. In no case, therefore, had she committed a crime. Perceiving that the newspapers were violently against her, she determined to get her points before her jury by speaking in every postal district of Monroe County. Such an effect had her words that the district attorney applied for a change of venue and obtained it. The trial was removed to Canandaigua, on the Finger Lakes in Ontario County.

The district attorney may have rubbed his hands, since there remained only a couple of weeks before the trial. But Susan Anthony immediately started a fresh canvass of Ontario County. Luckily for her, she was joined at last by a single helper, so that her case was once more placed before the people.

This sensational trial opened on a fine, sunny day in a pleasant rural courthouse before Judge Hunt, a pale, prim-looking man who was a recent appointee to the bench and evidently anxious to repay his political patrons for the favor. Miss Anthony attended, supported only by her sister and five of her friends. From the start it was obvious that the government had determined on conviction. The district attorney moved that a woman was incompetent to testify before the court. The judge upheld this, depriving Miss Anthony of the right to speak in her own defense. When her lawyer had done his best and the moment for summing up came, the judge produced from his pocket a paper which had been drawn up before he heard the case. The gist of this was that Miss Anthony was not protected by her belief that the law upheld her views. This being so, and since she did vote, she was admittedly guilty. There was no question left to put to the jury. Judge Hunt therefore dismissed the jury unheard and condemned Miss Anthony.

So far the prearranged plan had gone off smoothly. Here, however, Judge Hunt made a mistake. Turning to Miss An-thony, he asked her in the conventional way whether she had anything to say before he passed sentence. Burning with indig-nation, Miss Anthony certainly had. Vainly the judge attempted to forbid her to make a speech. In a few trenchant words, she brushed aside this travesty of justice. When he pronounced a hundred-dollar fine, she replied defiantly that she would never pay a penny of it.

Miss Anthony had the last word, for the judge was too pru-dent to commit her to jail for contempt of court; while the government was too wise to collect its hundred dollars. Arrest of Miss Anthony would have entitled her to appeal, and it was by no means obvious that the proceedings of the judge could have been upheld. Having made its own position clear, the government merely waited until the Supreme Court rejected the women's appeals already before it.

The crusade had failed in its object, but the way Miss An-thony had been treated won for her the sympathy her original act had not produced. Even conservative papers expressed out-rage. Letters and money for defense expenses came pouring in. Indeed, it now began to be noticeable that Miss Anthony was a popular figure, even though the political world was cold to her cause. The following year a newspaper called her America's best-known woman. As it pointed out, one had only to print *Susan,* and everybody knew who was intended. Hitherto Susan Anthony had been caricatured in the press as a mannish spinster working out her frustrations in extravagant ways. Starting in the early seventies, however, and increasing throughout her later career, she grew into one of America's best-loved women.

Even enemies soon had to be careful how they spoke of her.
Several factors contributed to this truly remarkable change.

The collapse of the *Revolution* in 1870 had left Miss Anthony
ten thousand dollars in debt. It was a crushing burden for a
woman without means and of no fixed income. Luckily for her,
a way of earning money had opened up. The rapid development
of communications and the ferment of ideas thrown up by the
war had resulted in an almost universal desire for information.
Public entertainments were still rare. Traveling theaters were
not acceptable to the more pious. But churches and congrega-
tions were ready for secular self-improvement. Lecture bureaus
had arisen to plan tours for prominent people, and Elizabeth
Stanton had seized on a chance to earn a college education for
her children. She introduced Susan to the lecture circuit; and
presently both were hard at work. Mrs. Stanton traveled eight
months in the year, but Susan Anthony was in almost perpetual
motion.

Elizabeth Stanton made an ideal lecturer. She was amiably
ready to talk on a variety of topics besides suffrage, such as home
life, great women of the Bible, or bringing up a family of boys.
On every subject she had original and interesting views. Besides, the charm of Elizabeth Stanton lay in motion, expression,
and wit. She was at her best with an audience. Those who loved
Susan Anthony were attracted by more personal qualities, chiefly
her selflessness and her endless interest in other people's problems. In public she was, inescapably, a battle-axe, blunt but con-
vincing. Her agents, capitalizing on her quality, hailed her in
their advance posters as "The Invincible."

Up and down the country The Invincible went, year in and
year out, keeping up with itineraries that made no provision for
missed connections, snowstorms, colds in the head, or other
accidents of nature. In twenty years, her agents later boasted,
she was forced to cancel only two engagements.

Lecture bureaus, paid out of a percentage of the takings, were
anxious to fill up their lecturers' time. Their employees in
consequence had to travel by day and night, change trains at

Susan B. Anthony, *(left)*, aged 55, and Elizabeth Cady Stanton, aged 60. At this age they were both lecturing all over the United States. *(Culver Pictures)*

odd hours, rush straight from a dusty journey onto a lecture platform. Elizabeth Stanton writes of giving a lecture, having a late supper and packing, taking a short nap on a sofa, being called at 2 A.M. and driven to the station in a mule cart through a fearful snowstorm, "the wind cutting like particles of glass." Her escort left her beside a red-hot stove in a waiting room, where she learned that the train was two hours late. She rolled up her cloak for a pillow and went to sleep, "listening to a discussion in an adjoining room on the merits of my lecture." When called, she transferred to the train and "flopped" asleep again without so much as taking off her bonnet. Miss Anthony came on her unexpectedly on one such occasion asleep on a railroad bench in Columbus, Ohio, while she waited for a train, "her gray curls sticking out." Susan Anthony passed from her fifties into her sixties at this work. Her seventies found her still at it. Elizabeth Stanton was five years older. They were veterans by now, and woman suffrage was a long way off.

It was drudgery, not particularly well paid. Earnings from a lecture varied from a couple of hundred down to thirty dollars, but expenses were high. Susan Anthony's earnings all went to pay her debt or to support her cause. Friends soon discovered it was no use giving her money for herself. Never did she buy so much as a book that she wanted. Her personal self-indulgences can be counted on the fingers of one hand: a couple of cheap brooches, a watch she greatly needed, and a pair of point-lace cuffs to match a collar given her by a friend.

In 1876, the crippling debt was paid off. All the papers noted the fact and did justice to Miss Anthony's heroic effort. The truth was, her public appearances and those of Elizabeth Stanton were disarming prejudice all over the country. The very sight of Mrs. Stanton gave the lie to lurid stories about woman reformers. Motherly, plump, always elegantly dressed, she was not conceivable in the role of a masculine woman. One could hardly associate her white curls or her descriptions of her full and happy family life with free love. Susan Anthony, though the very picture of a strong-minded spinster, had a natural nobility of bearing which grew on her with age. All those who gave her hospitality learned to like her; devotion increased with better acquaintance. Her consideration for others was a byword. In 1885, she traveled to Kansas with two small trunks instead of the conventional round-topped affair, leather-bound and massive, which ladies customarily used. She was asked to pay extra for the second trunk. Miss Anthony, to whom such expenses were a serious item, protested, pointing out that her two small trunks weighed less than the usual big one. She packed her luggage in this way, she said, to save the porter who had to do the lifting.

Railway officials were incredulous. Those were days in which manual labor was cheaply hired and not highly regarded. It had never occurred to them that anyone, least of all a female, would consider the porter.

"How long have you been doing this?" they asked her, astounded.

"All my life," replied Miss Anthony simply.

While her personal popularity increased, she also began to get better publicity. Reporters enjoyed her frankness and lack of temperamental airs. She could talk to them without affectation. Even the opposition was forced to admire her character and courage. Nothing ever dismayed her. "Only once in all these wanderings," says Elizabeth Stanton, "was Miss Anthony taken by surprise, and that was on being asked to speak to the inhabitants of an insane asylum. 'Bless me!' said she, 'it is as much as I can do to talk to the sane.' "

As Miss Anthony's fame increased, the National suffrage group prospered in her shadow. Less well organized than the American group, the National had started with few friends. The American, strong in state organizations, sought advancement mainly at that level. In big state campaigns Miss Anthony also threw her forces into the fray. Chiefly, however, the National put pressure directly on Congress. Susan Anthony had made fast friends with the proprietors of the Riggs Hotel in Washington, who for many years offered her free quarters. Freed from the burden of debt, she lightened somewhat her load of lectures and

Susan B. Anthony at her "desk with pigeonholes."
(*Culver Pictures*)

made Washington her headquarters for part of the year. Here the National Association held annual conventions while Congress was sitting. Miss Anthony with patient persistence made herself known in the lobbies.

Lobbying was dreary work. Miss Anthony generally got along well with men. Her business, however, was to make herself tiresome to friends and enemies alike. She pestered people at the Capitol or in their own homes. If they fobbed her off with promises for the future, she was present to be sure they carried them out. One senator, friendly but evasperated, wrote to her:

"I thought just as likely as not you would come fussing around before I got your amendment reported to the Senate. I wish you would go home. Cokrell has agreed to let me know soon whether he won't allow the report to be made right off without any bother, and I have been to him several times before. I don't see what you want to meddle for, anyway. Go off and get married!"

When her friends wrote in this strain, the comments of her enemies may well be imagined. But by her persistent efforts, the Anthony Amendment—drafted of course by Mrs. Stanton, but pushed by Miss Anthony—achieved committee hearings. It even received a favorable report and one vote on the floor of the Senate. There was no question of a majority in either house for the measure. At every party convention, Miss Anthony tried in vain to get a plank adopted favoring woman suffrage. The South was violently against the measure, preferring to keep white women voteless rather than to enfranchise colored women. The Republican North was repelled by an alliance between woman suffrage and the Temperance movement which was beginning to make itself felt. Neither party was willing to double the number of voters without being certain of gaining a party advantage. Yet as the eighties wore on, the Anthony Amendment ceased to seem the wild suggestion of a radical group. It had behind it a respectable body of sentiment and had to be treated as a practical proposition.

This much Miss Anthony had achieved in forty years. The National Suffrage Association held its annual conventions in Washington and was becoming prominent there. Clara Barton lent it the authority of her support. Miss Anthony had acquired during these years a handsome red shawl, not purchased of course, but given in memory of a dear, dead friend. This red shawl, "like the robin," as one reporter remarked, made its regular appearance in Washington every new year, becoming almost as famous in official circles as the harbinger of spring. Indeed, after some twenty years, when Miss Anthony appeared on a platform in a white shawl, the reporters sent up a scribbled note, "No red shawl, no report." Miss Anthony laughed and sent for her old one to please the "boys." She and the reporters were all good friends by now. But endless work still loomed ahead, and she was growing older.

5

The Woman's
Movement Covers the Nation
1869–1900

⁌

In 1869 Mrs. Esther Morris was a rugged-looking, six-foot woman in her middle fifties who had recently come to Wyoming with her husband and three sons. Two years earlier gold had been discovered at South Pass City, which was now a settlement of two or three thousand and the largest town in the Territory. In true western style, South Pass City was a hard-drinking, free-shooting place, many of whose inhabitants were merely stopping over to pan for a little gold on their way to California. Hardy, sensible, and self-reliant, Esther Morris had run a successful shop in Oswego, New York, moved on to Wyoming, and had in a few months made her mark in South Pass City.

It chanced that 1869 was the year in which the government of the Territory of Wyoming was formally established. The first elections were due to be held and the polling was expected, like everything else in Wyoming, to be rowdy. Before it took place, Esther Morris invited a group of community leaders together and appealed to them to grant women the vote. Mrs. Morris's arguments were neither more nor less sound than those of Susan B. Anthony, from whom she had derived them. The difference was that they prevailed. In the pioneer West, old prejudices wore faint. Men and women were tested alike under hard conditions, and the weak were not all of one sex. Esther Morris's guests agreed to support her cause; among them was William H. Bright, soon to become president of the first Wyoming territorial council.

William Bright was a self-educated man whose boast was that he had never had a single day of schooling. "Where I learned to read and write," he used to say, "I do not know." Although uncultured, he possessed immense energy. His wife was a superior woman whom he greatly admired. She too was a convert to the arguments of Esther Morris. Under her influence, Bright set to work on the Council and House of Representatives of the Territory, whose total membership was only twenty-two. The governor, he pointed out, was a bachelor and would certainly veto a woman suffrage bill. The Democrats could embarrass him by passing one, since he was a Republican. The Republicans, on the other hand, need not leave to the Democrats the kudos of bringing in so liberal a measure. Since it was certain not to become law, they might vote for it too.

Bright's energies prevailed in the party confusion of those early days in Wyoming. Before the horrified opposition had time to organize, his tactics had actually passed the bill in both houses. The governor was now expected to kill the measure. It happened, however, that twenty years earlier he had sat in the audience of a woman's rights convention in Salem, Ohio, and had concluded that the women's case was a perfectly reasonable one. He signed the bill.

Fearful predictions were now made that when women descended in hordes on the polling booths, fights would break out. Indeed, the scenes at Wyoming's preceding election had been such that women might reasonably be afraid to appear. In Laramie, however, Grandma Swain, a Quaker lady of seventy-five, marched into the polling booth first thing "to set an example." She was followed by other women, alone or with their husbands. None was molested. Both parties were anxious for the female vote and in consequence made it their business to control the men. Elections went off smoothly and resulted in changes in favor of good government. Women were less disposed to put up with rough riding and shooting. They hated the saloons and were not in the habit of getting drunk on election day. It was soon discovered that an election campaign need not depend on popularity in bars.

In 1890 Wyoming became a state. Pressure was applied in Washington to force repeal of the woman suffrage law. Wy-

Scene at the polls in Cheyenne, Wyoming Territory, when women first voted in 1869. (*Culver Pictures*)

oming leaders replied that they would rather stay out of the Union a hundred years than come in without the women. Thus the first woman suffrage state was admitted to the Union.

Utah, meanwhile, had made a similar effort. In 1870 there was a bill before Congress to outlaw the Mormon custom of plural marriage. Woman suffrage gave the Territory a chance to prove that its women were behind the institution. However, in 1887 Congress outlawed plural marriage and revoked the woman suffrage law in Utah Territory. Not until 1896 was Utah admitted to statehood with a provision for woman suffrage. By that time, Colorado and Idaho had joined the suffrage states, while various others had granted limited suffrage for such things as bond issues or school boards. Starting in the far West, suffrage was on the march.

These moderate successes were a sign that woman suffrage was beginning to make a serious impact on the nation. They were due in part to the persistence of Miss Anthony, the *Woman's Journal,* and the two rival suffrage associations. How-

"The Age of Brass, or the Triumph of Woman's Rights." An artist's comment on the introduction of votes for women in Wyoming in 1869. (*Culver Pictures*)

ever, a third organization had entered the field, more or less the
creation of one of America's supremely able women.

Frances Elizabeth Willard, born in 1839, was a descendant of
a long line of Puritan ancestors. The ambition of her father,
Josiah Willard, was to enter the ministry. Falling ill with tuberculosis, however, he was forced to choose an outdoor life and
settled on a Wisconsin farm, where Frances Willard spent eleven
years of childhood and adolescence. She was nine years old before she could write her name and fifteen before she had a real
teacher or entered a schoolhouse. Josiah Willard was an intensely religious man, a disciplinarian, and an old-fashioned
believer in the rights of the man of the house. He decided
everything at home, even choosing his daughters' dresses and
dismissing as vanity their desire to be consulted. His son was
sent away to school and college, but a little music and good
domestic training were plenty for girls. Frances Willard's girlhood is the story of a persistent struggle for freedom hidden
under the cloak of a religion she thought she accepted—and in
part did always accept. Thus when she was able to break away,
she took with her a cloud of pious sentiments and a vocabulary
well fitted to soften the effect of daring thoughts.

She had always envied her brother and wanted to be a boy.
Her mother, seeing that she did not care for household tasks,
let her do as she liked. Her father's puritanical ways made normal relations with young men almost impossible. She consoled
herself, therefore, by a series of ardent friendships with other
girls which taught her to play on women's hearts. With one of
these friends she was enabled to spend two years in Europe,
traveling and educating herself. She returned to America
broadened, even cultured, yet with the same sentimental ver-
biage as before. She was wildly ambitious, determined not merely
to do good, but also to be recognized as great, to be served and
adored. She took the presidency of a new woman's college which
shortly merged with Northwestern. But as dean of women she
could not get on with her male board, nor they with her. For
all her abilities, she was never easy in second place. She resigned,

collapsing in a storm of hysterical tears, and was free to take the chance fate soon offered.

These were the years immediately following the Civil War. The position of women had been permanently altered during that struggle and was still changing fast. Gas lighting, efficient stoves, commercial canning and manufactured shoes, the invention of the sewing machine were giving the housewife more leisure. The influx of immigrant girls made servants easy to get. A great many women had found that these changes in domestic habits gave them time to be useful in the war. They had knitted, made bandages, raised money for medicines, and had formed committees for such purposes, encouraged by their husbands and their pastors. In fact, they had discovered an interest in good works and a power of accomplishment they had not previously known that they possessed. Now that the emergency was over, they were unwilling to retire into seclusion. Nor were the clergy, always influential over women, entirely anxious that they should. Women had proved that they could be useful without interfering with male superiority in the home. Their energy, if directed into acceptable channels, their pastors felt, must work for good.

The cause of Temperance had long been especially dear to female hearts because of the inadequacies of the law to protect women or children against the abuses of a drunken husband or father. As we have seen, male Temperance associations had been unfavorable to woman's advancement. But these were different days. A lady lecturer or a ladies' club was hardly even frowned on now. Coeducation, advancing rapidly in the schools, was penetrating to the college level. So long as a woman did not put herself forward with unreasonable claims of equality, most men were by now willing to concede her a sphere of her own.

Meanwhile, the production of liquor was benefiting largely from habits engendered by the war, from the arrival of poor and overworked immigrants from Europe, and from the government tax which, providing a useful part of revenue, gave the business a godfather in Uncle Sam. Problems of drunkenness increased in proportion. On the day before Christmas in 1873, a group of church women in Hillsboro, Ohio, decided to do something about them.

Electing a prominent churchwoman their leader, a hundred women marched out of the church in a long column, singing "Give the Wind Thy Fears," and made straight for the nearest saloon. Here they knelt down and prayed, inside and outside, asking the Lord to change the heart of its owner and direct him to seek some other form of business. Naturally there was an enormous sensation in Hillsboro. Everyone gathered to stare, many to laugh. But the women kept at it, encouraging one another by Bible readings and hymns when the flow of extempore prayer dried up. Presently in consternation this first saloon closed its doors, and the ladies passed on to another.

Local papers spread the sensational news. Washington Courthouse and Springfield in Ohio, Fredonia in New York caught the fever. Within a few months the leading eastern and midwestern states were aflame. The far West, too, was being stirred. No special leaders arose in what was essentially a local movement, and perhaps for this reason its popularity was surprisingly great. When prominent women of a community were willing to kneel all day on the dirty boards of a saloon, nobody was anxious to arrest them for trespass. It is different, as the twentieth-century civil rights movement has shown, when "outsiders" come in. Besides, local churches generally supported the women. Unfeminine their action might be, but it was certainly pious and humble. The clergy were active in Temperance work and could not logically show displeasure at the closing of saloons. Thus the Woman's War, as the press christened it, raged furiously throughout 1874, temporarily closing about three thousand saloons. Frances Willard, who had resigned that very June from Northwestern, showed interest in it.

Her convictions on Temperance were not very firm. She had taken a pledge in girlhood under the influence of her father's religion, but in Europe she had been perfectly ready to follow local customs about drinking wine with her meals. She hated saloons, to be sure, and did not drink strong liquor. Her interest in the Woman's War, however, was largely concerned with it as a woman's movement.

By the end of the summer, the Woman's War was dying out. Local leaders, who perceived that they could not go on praying forever, were anxious to establish permanent Temperance leagues. Frances Willard, whose position in the world of female education had been a distinguished one, was free and willing to become president of the Chicago organization. As such she was rapidly chosen as an Illinois delegate to a national meeting. This convention resulted in the formation of the Woman's National Christian Temperance Union.

The WCTU, as it came to be called, was a nonsectarian organization, though with a predominantly Methodist membership. It had the blessing of distinguished clergymen and yet was entirely without male members. Its feet were firmly on the local ground. Individual groups, formed during the period of the crusade, were at liberty to join the organization if they were willing to endorse the constitution and pay dues. These local unions elected delegates to a state association. It, in turn, sent representatives to a national council. This chose the president and officers of the movement, electing Frances Willard to the position of corresponding secretary.

The corresponding secretary of the WCTU was in a position almost as strategic as that of Stalin in the Communist hierarchy when Lenin died. She was not the president, but she was the person who had direct connections with the rank and file. The state organizations, coming in between the national and local groups, cut off the officers except for the corresponding secretary, whose business it was to close the gap. Thus Frances Willard, widely known and loved, soon found herself in a position to initiate policy.

Her first ideas merely consolidated what had already been won. A woman's movement had actually arisen with the blessing of the clergy and was composed of ordinary housewives who were not intending a female revolution. Frances Willard gave them a battle cry, "For God and Home and Native Land." It was the kind of cliché that appealed quite naturally to her and to her audience. She was a brilliant speaker of an emotional sort, and she made the slogan sound magnificent as she rolled it out, her small, neat, auburn-haired head flung back, her pince-nez shining, with the rapt smile on her face which fascinated so many. It was a romantic age, and these were its methods of expression. But Frances Willard was more than a spellbinder.

She deliberately set herself to define the purpose of the organization in terms wider than those of mere Temperance work. Presently she coined the expression "Home Protection," which pleased everybody. Women were glad to be told that they had invaded Temperance work in defense of their homes. This made action their plain duty, as church and husband must agree. Nothing could be more suitable to woman's traditional role than home protection. Most women saw no further than this, but to Frances Willard it was clear from the first that homes might be protected in ways other than working for temperance. In fact, a very great number of other reforms might be justified by that useful slogan. Thus, gathering her forces under a conservative banner, Frances Willard marched women out to fight for progress.

They did not know where they were heading. Frances Willard had decided that for prohibition, as for every other reform, women needed the vote. As she put it, "We need the Home Protection Ballot." Cautiously she introduced a resolution in Chicago "That we will pray and labor for the early dawning of that day when the mothers and daughters of America shall have a voice in the decision by which the door of the rum-shop is opened or shut beside their homes." Naturally a few perceived this was a suffrage resolution, but the majority of the Illinois state organization, hoodwinked by Frances Willard's impassioned eloquence, adopted it. Following up this initial success by propaganda in the WCTU official paper, she defended herself against opposition, claiming that even minority views had a right to be heard. In the course of about five years she had so undermined the position of the president, a conservative older woman, that she succeeded to the office herself. It was a victory of the Midwest over the East, of progress over conservatism, and of a tight organization over a loose one.

In 1879 Frances Willard became president of the WCTU, which was to remain her private empire until her death in 1898. She had early insisted that representation must depend on payment of dues and had won a victory over those who said praying was more important than paying. Thus she had behind her what was, for a woman's movement, a well-financed and formidable organization. Her talents directed, enlarged, and held it together.

The basis of her power was always emotional. She could make her audience laugh, cry, or cheer at will. She understood the effect of mass pageantry on people. She had a power of inspiring personal devotion that amounted almost to worship. Nor did she hesitate to use this for the cause. One may compare Frances Willard in her later years, magnificently housed by a friend in an English castle, attended by her faithful secretary-and-ladies'-maid, keeping six stenographers busy, with the naïve exclamation of Miss Anthony in 1895: "Why, bless him, I never, in all my fifty years of hard work with the pen, had a writing desk with pigeonholes and drawers until my seventieth birthday."

Although Frances Willard's appeal was emotional, her mind was clear. If she drove people, her own powers of work were phenomenal. Frances Willard was a real Napoleon disguised in the petticoats of a Sunday-school teacher. Before she had done with the WCTU, that innocuous phrase "Home Protection" covered nearly forty different departments of activity, including direct work for woman suffrage, a campaign against the white-slave traffic under a department of social purity, a department of health and hygiene, mothers' meetings, cooperative kindergartens, international peace propaganda, various forms of welfare work, temperance education in the public schools, and improvement of working conditions for women. She even established, on the pretext of a link between the factory and Temperance, a close connection between the WCTU and the Knights of Labor. Soaring higher yet, she attempted and nearly succeeded in a welding together of all reform organizations into the Populist party, which contended for political power in the nineties.

Under Miss Willard's leadership ordinary American women, too contented or too unimaginative to be stirred by the feminist movement, were swept into reform work by simply following the safe, religious path of home protection. The WCTU may fairly claim to be the first mass movement among American women. It provided the suffrage group with things it never had before—an abundance of workers in the local field, better financial backing, and a hold on the ordinary middle-class American woman. More important still, it achieved respectability for suffrage in the eyes of the church, of women themselves, and even of many men. For this, Miss Willard's emotion was far more serviceable than Mrs. Stanton's logic.

With such auxiliaries, it soon became possible to fight a real campaign in states, largely western, which suggested woman suffrage as a change in the state constitution. This involved a referendum, or in other words a direct appeal to voters on the question at the time of the next election. The statewide campaigns necessary on these occasions were expensive, and women had to do their work on a shoestring. State suffrage associations, too, were often weak. Busy women worked madly in a crisis but slackened off when it was past. Often their real interest was temperance, missionary charity, or some other form of WCTU work. Communications in the West were difficult also. Communities were small and far apart. But in spite of all difficulties, woman suffrage was a living issue in the West, where the example of Wyoming kept it before the public. Often rejected, it came up again and again.

The national associations were generous with money and time. When a referendum came up in South Dakota in 1890, Susan Anthony was seventy years old. Her health was not good. Conditions in Dakota were terribly primitive, and the summer was one of the hottest on record. She was urged to cancel her

trip. "Better lose me than lose a state," she replied. She went out
to Dakota and remained six months, turning down lucrative
offers of lectureships elsewhere. She spoke all over the state,
often driving twenty miles between morning and afternoon
meetings and sharing an attic bed in a two-room house at the
end of the day. But the Knights of Labor and the Farmers' Alliance, both of whom had invited her to campaign, merged into
the People's party and quietly dropped woman suffrage. Meanwhile, saloonkeepers, who thought woman suffrage meant
prohibition, did their utmost to defeat it. Marshaling the immigrants, of whom there were many in the state, thousands not
English-speaking and illiterate in any language, they led them
to the polls in drilled platoons and paid them off in full sight of
the poll-watchers for voting *No*.

The state was lost, and Miss Anthony was nearly lost as well.
But the real significance of the Dakota campaign was its revela-
tion of the tactics of the opposition. The façade of male superiority was crumbling fast, and everybody could see what lay
behind. Women's old grievances were being remedied everywhere. As a speaker put it in 1888:

"We know there have been great improvements in the laws
in regard to women. What brought about these improvements?
The steady labor of women like these on this platform, going
before legislatures year after year and asking for something
they were not willing to give, the ballot; but as a result of it, to
keep the poor creatures quiet, some law was passed removing a
restriction. The old English writer Pepys, according to his diary,
after spending a good deal of money for himself finds a little
left and buys his wife a new gown, because, as he says, 'It is fit
that the poor wretch should have something to content her.' "

The poor wretch took what she could get, while the suffrage
movement grew steadily throughout the eighties and nineties.
But the influence of Frances Willard was not entirely good,
since the WCTU had its own enemies. Liquor interests soon
identified woman suffrage with prohibition. As early as 1882,
the Brewers' Association sent orders to every saloon in Ne-

braska to fight against woman suffrage. By 1906, a secret circular by the brewers and wholesale liquor dealers of the state of Oregon said explicitly that it would take fifty thousand votes to defeat woman suffrage and there were two thousand retailers in the state. Each was therefore requested to produce twenty-five votes by putting pressure on his employees, grocer, butcher, landlord, laundryman, and others. Twenty-five ballot tickets were enclosed in each envelope, together with a post card addressed to the association which the retailer should mail when his twenty-five votes were assured.

Thus, as the suffrage associations grew, the opposition grew also, no longer consisting of the church and the conservative element, but of a big business controlling millions of dollars and a very large measure of political power. The conflict, in fact, had completely changed. The women now needed a high degree of political sophistication. Propaganda required funds. The California campaign of 1894, biggest of the century, may serve as an example of what the suffrage movement was becoming.

It opened under favorable auspices. Largely due to the eloquence of Miss Anthony and her able assistant Anna Shaw, the Republican party came out for suffrage. The Populists followed suit. Almost all the papers were in favor, and in the course of an eight-month campaign nine thousand clippings were obtained, an extraordinary number when it is remembered that local papers depended on advertising money, which was not available from the suffrage movement. Meanwhile, the California organization raised nineteen thousand dollars for expenses, much of it in tiny installments. Working women would drop in to pay twenty-five cents on a two-dollar photograph of Miss Anthony and Miss Shaw, remarking "I have done without tea this week," or "I made a piece of fancywork evenings and sold it." Susan Anthony gave her own time. She had lately afforded the modest expense of a secretary; and friends, mindful of her seventy-four years, had paid the secretary's way to California. She found herself working full time for the cause, while Miss Anthony, though speaking as often as three times a day, handled all her own vast correspondence.

Past experience had trained suffrage workers and a corps of able women speakers. California was deluged with literature, flooded with copies of the *Woman's Journal*. Miss Anthony made a campaign trip by train, stopping at every station for a ten-minute address, which she often delivered in the most thinly settled spots to as many as a thousand.

Meanwhile, the opposition was hard at work. The Republicans, under secret pressure, refused to supply speakers for the measure they had promised to support. The Populists, despairing of their own cause, combined with the Democrats and threw over woman suffrage in the process. The liquor dealers held a meeting in San Francisco to organize opposition. Frantic efforts were made to get out the immigrant vote against the women; advertisements were published appealing to them in every paper. Men were sent around ringing doorbells. Interpreters were employed to explain that voting costs nothing. Registration books were carried to places of employment. Miss Anthony well knew that a first or last amendment on a list was an easy target for the illiterate and had made a special appeal to have it put in the middle. The secretary of state assured her it should be placed third, but it came out last when the ballots were actually printed.

Deserted by their friends and powerfully opposed, Miss Anthony and her cohorts struggled on. But they were appealing to the women of the state rather than to the voters. At midnight on election day, she and a friend made a melancholy journey around San Francisco, "peering into the windows of the rough little booths where the judges and clerks of the election were counting votes. The rooms were black with tobacco smoke, and in one they saw a man fall off his chair too drunk to finish the count. They listened to the oaths and jeers as the votes were announced against the suffrage amendment to which they had given their lives." Then they crept away, to start preparing for next time.

6

Suffrage
Becomes Dull and Respectable
1884–1910

ℰ

In 1882, Miss Anthony and Mrs. Stone were each left a legacy
of twenty thousand dollars to devote to woman suffrage. The
will was contested, and it became necessary for them to agree on
measures. They met for the first time since 1869, and the ice
was broken between them. Throughout the eighties, it was
becoming obvious that the two suffrage organizations ought to
merge. State suffrage groups in the West, a long way from Boston
and Washington, found little difference between the American
and the National associations. Delegations were apt to be sent
to the conventions of both, while the two organizations, anxious
for members, were never firm enough to stop this process. The
aim of the two was admittedly the same. The American Association preferred to work through the states, while Susan Anthony
lobbied for a constitutional amendment. Yet when a state
campaign came up, the National and Miss Anthony flew into
the fray. Similarly, the more conservative American Association
was more likely to gather the fruit of Frances Willard's work
among conservative women. Yet Susan Anthony, who recognized quality wherever she saw it, was on excellent terms with
that remarkable woman.

Susan Anthony in person was the best argument for reunion.
She was clearly emerging as the outstanding figure in the movement. To America at large, woman suffrage simply meant
Susan. It was asking too much of the American Association that
it should continue to stand apart. Younger leaders had long
forgotten Train and Victoria Woodhull. They were attracted
to Miss Anthony by a natural process. Indeed, Anna Shaw, Miss

Anthony's assistant and closest friend during the nineties, came from the American not the National Association.

Anna Shaw had been born in England in 1847 to an impractical father who failed in business and brought his large brood to America. Here he took a factory job in New Bedford, Massachusetts, and then bought uncleared land in northern Michigan. Going out there with his eldest son, he cut and burned a few acres on which he put up a log cabin. In this primitive shack he installed his wife and children while he returned to New Bedford to earn money. Anna was twelve at that time. Her older brother fell ill and had to go back East. Her two next brothers had been taken by her father. Her mother soon became an invalid, unable to stand without support. Anna had two small sisters to help her and her brother Harry, eight years old, when they arrived in Michigan. Father sent remittances as he could and abolitionist tracts. They were a hundred miles from the railroad, forty miles from a post office, and six miles from their nearest neighbors. Somehow they lived, while Anna performed the hardest manual labor and educated herself as Lincoln had done.

The Civil War came, and the men of the family enlisted. Anna, now drudging away as a schoolteacher, supported the rest. Only after the war did she get a chance at high school and discovered in herself the gift of eloquence. Presently she was asked by a Methodist minister to preach. After some heart-searchings she did and soon desired to be ordained. This involved an outright quarrel with the family which owed her so much. Unassisted, she starved her way through theological school, existing once for a whole week on a box of crackers. Called to a parish on Cape Cod, she found the quiet, rural life too easy. Besides, she began to feel that it was useless to heal men's souls as long as their bodies were shamefully neglected. She went to Boston and entered medical school. In 1885, she gained her M.D. By then experience in the Boston slums had convinced her that the basic problem was beyond both religion and medicine. Laws must be made and enforced. She began to lecture for the WCTU on temperance and to work in its suffrage department. This introduced her to the American suffrage group, which hired her for a small sum as a part-time speaker.

The Reverend Doctor Shaw was immediately conspicuous. Indeed, throughout her later career she was widely recognized as the most eloquent speaker of her times. Acquainted with Frances Willard, she soon got to know Miss Anthony, who was always on the lookout for coming talent. Miss Anthony urged her to devote her full time to suffrage work. Dr. Shaw resisted. She had to earn her bread, and suffrage hardly ever paid. But Miss Anthony persisted.

In 1888 the two found themselves together at a conference in Chicago. Anna was already in bed, propped up on pillows, when Miss Anthony appeared for an evening talk. She had been too busy to eat dinner and possibly had had no lunch. Now she was too keyed up to sleep. She began to tell Anna about her plans, dwelling, as her habit was, not on the past but on the future. It was like hearing a general outline his campaigns for years ahead. Anna listened and questioned. Miss Anthony, relaxed with a confidante of her own caliber, talked on.

Neither of the women thought of sleep. The moment was among the most thrilling of Anna's life. All night Miss Anthony dissected suffrage problems till the gas jets grew pale in the morning light and found her still talking. She stopped and looked surprised, but recovered herself. She threw off the rug over her knees and got up. "I must dress now," she said. "I've called a committee meeting before the morning session."

As she turned to the door "nature smote her with a rare reminder," says Anna Shaw. After all, Miss Anthony was sixty-eight, had hardly eaten the day before, and had not slept. But she was not accustomed to considering herself and did not realize her own fatigue. She turned back to Anna Shaw, one hand on the door. "Perhaps," she remarked tentatively, "you ought to have a cup of coffee."

After that occasion, Anna Shaw devoted her entire time to suffrage work and became Miss Anthony's right hand. Affectionate, vigorous, and outgoing, she soon established a lively intimacy with her. Earlier young workers had already baptized Miss Anthony "Aunt Susan." When Anna Shaw became an honorary niece, the merger of the two suffrage groups into one National-American Association could not be long delayed. It followed in 1889, negotiated largely by Alice Stone Blackwell, only child of Lucy's marriage. Thus the younger generation imposed peace upon their elders.

Lucy Stone and Miss Anthony were willing to be reconciled. Mrs. Stone did suggest that old rivalries be buried by an agreement that she, Miss Anthony, and Mrs. Stanton should all refuse the office of president. Such an arrangement, however, was unthinkable. No national suffrage movement could be formed without Miss Anthony at the head, while she, as usual, insisted on Mrs. Stanton's right to be the leader. Both the National Association, which looked to Miss Anthony, and the American, which feared Mrs. Stanton's exuberance, were reluctant to accept this arrangement; but Susan Anthony was all-powerful. She was given the title of vice-president at large. Mrs. Stanton presided.

It was well for the conservative members of the American Association that Mrs. Stanton had for years been less active in the suffrage movement. Her lecture tours and growing family had consumed much time. In 1880, she had retired from lecturing at the age of sixty-five and proposed to take life easy. She suggested to Susan that they skip the annual convention of the National Association—it had been a busy year—and told her to write to the treasurer on the subject. The treasurer's protest got an answer from Miss Anthony: "I wrote you under Mrs. Stanton's orders not to tell you how I felt. . . . She won't promise to attend, she never does, but I never fail to take her with me when I am on the spot, as I shall be when the time comes."

Presently Mrs. Stanton made herself more inaccessible still. She was now widowed and made her home with her daughter Harriot Blatch, who had married an Englishman and lived in

Elizabeth Cady Stanton in old age. (*Brown Brothers*)

England. In 1888, when a great international conference which she and Miss Anthony had conceived was coming up, she wrote in excellent spirits of attending. Soon, however, she decided that she could not face the long sea voyage. "I wrote the most terrific letter to Mrs. Stanton," says Susan Anthony. "It will start every white hair in her head." In response, Mrs. Stanton came—but without a speech ready. She had to be literally imprisoned in the Riggs Hotel with a guard at her door to turn away intrusive friends. When the time came, she rose to the occasion with her old magnificence. But it was obvious that the most she would often do as president of the National-American was send over speeches which Miss Anthony would dutifully read at annual meetings.

On these terms, the National-American accepted Mrs. Stanton for a few years. In 1892, however, she resigned. Lucy Stone died. Susan Anthony remained president of the movement she had led for so long. Her activity was still phenomenal, her popularity immense. Not only was she surrounded by her adoring "nieces," but the general public had taken her to its heart. In spite of adulation, she remained the same unspoiled Susan Anthony. At the age of eighty-six she was being ushered into a large meeting when the audience burst into cheers at the sight of her figure. Puzzled, she glanced around, then whispered into the ear of her escort to find out what they were applauding. It was not surprising that all who worked with Miss Anthony learned to love her.

From 1892 to 1900 Miss Anthony held the presidency, laying it down when she was eighty years of age. In a superficial way the nineties were successful years for suffrage. Two states were won. Two territories which had had suffrage before were admitted to the Union. Yet these four states were small and not influential. The liquor interests were organizing in powerful opposition. Meanwhile the policy of the American Association, to win suffrage state by state, was beginning to prevail in the united movement. State organizations were becoming stronger, and they naturally preferred to work on their own ground.

Besides, the proprietors of the Riggs Hotel in Washington had retired and were unable to offer Miss Anthony free headquarters. She therefore retreated to her family home in Rochester, which she shared with her unmarried sister. Here she rested after campaigns and conventions. Here she kept in touch and summoned executive meetings. But she could not keep pressure on Congress from Rochester. Congressional hearings soon sank to an annual farce, while the National-American poured its efforts into state campaigns and state propaganda.

It was time for Miss Anthony to retire. She saw it herself. No question of actually ceasing to work ever entered her head. Her reputation, for what it was worth, was at the service of her movement. But someone else must take the load. Her own personal preference was clearly for Anna Shaw, marked out by energy, eloquence, and her close relationship with dear Aunt Susan. But personal preferences do not count, and another contender of a different sort was coming into the limelight.

Carrie Chapman Catt had been born Carrie Lane in 1859. Her father had moved from New York State to Ripon, Wisconsin, and thence to Charles City, Iowa. Carrie, a precocious child, insisted on high school and wanted to go on to college. Her father did not agree. Carrie decided to earn her college money and, making all arrangements, faced him with the fact that she had already gained the teachers' certificate and had landed a contract to teach in her own district school for the following winter.

She chose Iowa State College at Ames because it was cheap and, soon after graduating, married Leo Chapman, young editor of the Mason City *Republican*. Perceiving her talents, he used her as assistant editor. It was while she was in this position that she took up a petition to the legislature on municipal suffrage for women, so organizing Mason City that every woman except a couple of dozen signed her paper. The state suffrage association, which was affiliated with the American Association, was startled to recognize such ability in their midst. They invited

Carrie to a convention in Cedar Rapids, where she met Lucy
Stone and was vividly impressed by her simple determination.
But before Carrie could make her mark in Iowa, fate snatched
her away. Leo Chapman, ambitious to better himself, sold the
Republican and prepared to move to California. In fact, he went
on ahead to look around and possibly buy a newspaper there.
Within a few weeks he was dead of typhoid, leaving Carrie to
go out and arrange his funeral.

She stayed in San Francisco after that and took a job on a
paper. As a proprietor's widow she got a certain amount of
respect, but she saw other women overworked, underpaid, restricted to menial jobs. Resentment hardened. Presently her
employer asked her to leave a message with a businessman on
her way home. She went up to his office and found that his staff
had already left. He, seeing himself alone with a young and
personable woman who was going about without a male protector, took advantage of his opportunity. He grabbed her.

"Gimme a kiss!"

Disgusted and furious, she fought him off and made her way
to the street. But the humiliation of the episode determined
her. There had been other slights, but this was the last straw.
She would not tolerate an inferior position in a man's world.
She would go back to Iowa, lecture to earn her bread, and work
for the emancipation of women.

By 1890, Carrie was a delegate to the first convention of the
new National-American. She attracted notice. Carrie Chapman
was tall and well formed with soft brown hair, good features,
and a noble presence. Her speech was slow, deliberate, and impressive. Her mind was startlingly incisive. She pledged her
service in the South Dakota campaign, the one that nearly killed
Miss Anthony. It even more nearly killed Carrie Chapman, who
came down with typhoid and almost succumbed. But she had
proved her worth. Miss Anthony had tested her in the hardest
of circumstances, and she did not fail.

George Catt, an old college friend, was now an engineer living in Seattle, but moving about a good deal. He had been

courting Carrie Chapman ever since her San Francisco days and did not see that her devotion to a cause should interfere with marriage. In fact, like Henry Blackwell, he proposed to do the earning for both, while she did the public work. He went to the length of having a written contract drawn up which allowed her two months in the spring and two in the fall for suffrage speaking.

On these terms Carrie married George Catt, and the partnership proved happy. But unlike Henry Blackwell, George Catt did not make a competence and retire. He made a fortune, first in the Far West, then in New York. Carrie, though never diverted from suffrage work, found herself a rich man's wife, moving in circles far more worldly than those of Lucy Stone or Susan Anthony. Perhaps for this reason, Miss Anthony never completely took her to her heart. Mentally and in powers of organization the two were alike. Mrs. Catt, however, was a politician, at her best a statesman, rather than a general. Although not without warmth, she was no enthusiast like Dr. Shaw. Her convictions sprang from the mind rather than from the heart.

In 1894 a referendum on the question of woman suffrage came up in Colorado, which the national organization did not consider important. There was a campaign for municipal suffrage in Kansas, another in New York. The Colorado bill was not supported by the major political parties, and the women's national treasury was not inexhaustible. Miss Anthony directed her efforts elsewhere, leaving Colorado to the efforts of Mrs. Catt.

This policy paid an unexpected dividend. Opposition forces, reasoning as Miss Anthony had done, concentrated their efforts where she did. Nobody quite realized that an organizer of matchless ability with personal knowledge of the West had taken Colorado in hand. The bill was passed, and Colorado joined the suffrage states.

This success of course enhanced Mrs. Catt's reputation. Meanwhile, at the annual national convention early in 1895, Miss

Anthony appointed Mrs. Catt to chair a committee to plan for the coming year. Two days later Mrs. Catt arose to make her report. Suffrage agitation, she pointed out, had failed to organize the sentiment it had created. Suffrage needed to correlate its national, state, and local branches, to set out concrete aims, to have a finance committee that would really work on finance. Meantime, she proposed a standing committee on organization which should put organizers in the field, each traveling with a business manager. It should plan regional conferences midway between the big conventions. It should draw up a course in politics and government for the use of local clubs, investigate the different local laws about women and children, inquire into property owned and taxes paid by women. It should in fact endeavor to systematize a chaotic mass of material and see that the relevant parts of it got into the hands of people who could use them. Finally she apologized for being sketchy and mildly suggested that a planning committee ought to meet a few weeks in advance of a convention.

Somewhat stunned by the sweeping nature of these proposals, the convention lost no time in elevating Mrs. Catt to the presidency of an organization committee. She found herself, as was usual in the movement, in charge of a tremendous job with no office and no money except what she could raise herself. After three weeks she hired a stenographer. After two months the secretary of the committee came permanently to stay. By the end of the year, these three women had sent out seven thousand letters and used three quarts of ink. They had started a shopping agency which turned in its commissions and a suffrage calendar to earn money over Christmas. They had raised and spent over five thousand dollars, turned Mrs. Catt's home into an office, kept fourteen organizers in the field, and brought every state and territory into the association, including ten states with no previous organization.

By the following year the Organization Committee had opened a New York office, which was soon absorbing a great deal of the work of national headquarters, theoretically located in a private home in Philadelphia. The committee was drawing up instruction booklets for officers of suffrage clubs. It was compiling a directory of clubs. Previously no one had known how many there were of these and how they were run. Meanwhile, recruitment went briskly on. In 1896, the committee ran conventions in each of the ninety-nine counties in Iowa, having two teams of organizers conducting meetings in adjoining counties so that speakers could be exchanged. The whole was wound up by a state convention in Des Moines, where a headquarters was opened to press for a state suffrage law. Similar treatment was given South Dakota and Illinois. Idaho was actually won. Mrs. Catt demanded more funds, and Miss Anthony backed her up, producing eight hundred dollars, none quite knew how, from her own meager resources.

The power of the Organization Committee grew mightily; and when Miss Anthony retired in 1900, Mrs. Catt was as logical a choice for the succession as Dr. Shaw. She had, moreover, one great advantage. Dr. Shaw was dependent on her lecture earnings. Mrs. Catt had money and could therefore give her whole time to the movement. Ever more clearly for the last five years, the Organization Committee had proved that pioneer days had gone by. Short of a good salary—still not to be thought of—the president of the suffrage movement needed resources.

These considerations were bound to prevail. Miss Anthony was sad, since she dearly loved Anna Shaw; but she understood that Mrs. Catt must be her successor. Anna Shaw herself, though disappointed, was above jealousy. Miss Anthony laid down the reins, and Mrs. Catt assumed them.

For the next few years, Mrs. Catt organized with considerable success. State officers matured rapidly under the new regime. Finances assumed a more prosperous look. But no more suffrage states had yet been added. Mrs. Catt had seen voters paid at the polls in South Dakota. In Arizona, legislators had broken a promise of support sooner than have their businesses ruined. A referendum in New Hampshire required a midwinter campaign. Mrs. Catt moved up to Concord, importing fifteen speakers, and opened an office where she spent five days of the week, speaking on weekends. She plowed through snow to the knee and rode in sleighs hugging hot soapstones, to no avail. Everyone told her quite calmly that elections in New Hampshire must be paid for. She was up against big business, organized crime, and the whole political structure of the male world. All of these had interests adverse to woman suffrage, and untraceable connections ran from one to the other. The dimensions of the problem, in fact, had now become plain. Not even the brilliance of Mrs. Catt had found an answer.

Meanwhile, she faced her own problems. Organizers are apt to make enemies, and Mrs. Catt was no exception. She had to sacrifice her Organization Committee. Her health was only fairly good, by no means equal to the strains that Miss Anthony had put on hers. Worse still, George Catt was increasingly ill. In 1904, Carrie told the organization that she could not go on. Her husband, who had made her work possible, needed her attention. She resigned to take him abroad. Dr. Shaw, now the only possible president, was duly elected.

Miss Anthony lived to see her favorite's triumph, but not long enough to perceive that it would do harm. She died at the age of eighty-six, and Rochester turned out in a body to pay respects to its greatest citizen. The presidency of Dr. Shaw was not overshadowed by Miss Anthony, and it would have been easy for her to put forward constructive ideas.

The popularity of Miss Anthony during the eighties and nineties had partly obscured the fact that she was becoming out of date. For all the greatness of her personality, Miss Anthony was a small-town farmer's daughter with a narrow education, still running a nationwide organization by shoestring methods. During the last years of her reign, state organizations asserted themselves increasingly against her. This was a healthy sign, or would have been so under fresh leadership. Dr. Shaw, Miss Anthony's "niece" and friend, with similarly narrow background, brought to her task an earnest desire to do good. She looked, however, backward, actually suspicious of suggestions.

Harriot Stanton Blatch, returning widowed from England in
1907, regarded the movement her mother had founded with a
disillusioned eye. Suffrage was respectable and dull. It preached
largely to the converted. Little booklets were sent out to suffrage clubs from headquarters, which were no longer in New
York, but in Warren, Ohio, where the treasurer of the movement chanced to live. The corresponding secretary was in New
Orleans. Dr. Shaw, near Philadelphia, kept in touch with her
executive committee by mail. Letters went back and forth, in-
conclusive and irritating. Nothing got done.

The federal amendment, meanwhile, was perfectly dead. Few
state referenda had come up, and none of these had looked like
winning. "Educate and organize," suffrage leaders parroted.
But for what? Nearly every well-meaning person seemed to believe in woman suffrage, and yet nobody cared much about the
issue. Carrie Chapman Catt years before had put her finger
on this problem:

"The chief obstacle is not found in societies opposed to the
extension of suffrage to women, nor in ignorance, nor in conservatism; it is to be found in that large body of suffragists who
believe that the franchise will come, but that it will come in
some unaccountable way without effort or concern on their
part."

Suffrage seemed to have reached a dead stop. Meanwhile, however, the number of woman college graduates was rising. The
number of wage-earning women was rising also. The invention
of the typewriter had given women a position in industry less
menial than that of the seamstress or factory hand. As their
position improved, women's need of fair legislation grew greater.
Their fitness for suffrage was becoming indisputable. It was
enthusiasm which was lacking.

7
New Leadership
1905–1912

A blood transfusion was needed. It came, surprisingly, from England. The suffrage movement there, which had gone through various phases, had entered the twentieth century in a moribund state when it was suddenly revived by Mrs. Emmeline Pankhurst, widow of a prominent Manchester barrister. She was a frail, enthusiastic, spirited creature who out of admiration had married a man many years her senior. Dr. Pankhurst had been a tireless fighter for liberal causes, finding plenty of windmills to tilt at in the ugly commercial town of Manchester with its smug prosperity, its dingy slums, its knot of liberals, and its rising working-class leaders. He had worn himself out at last, leaving Emmeline in her middle forties with two daughters, Christabel and Sylvia, just growing up. She had shared her husband's enthusiasms, which included woman suffrage. His death had deprived her of a chance to fight for most of them, but the suffrage issue could be taken up by any woman. Mrs. Pankhurst, who now more than ever needed a cause, adopted it.

The problem of the suffragists in England was in some ways simpler than that of those in America. There were no forty-eight states to convert—merely Parliament. But the tyranny of a parliamentary majority is absolute. There could be no question of passing a measure unless it were adopted by the party in power. So far all efforts had made not the slightest impression on Conservative or Liberal politicians.

Mrs. Pankhurst, trained by her husband in the tough school of Manchester politics, tossed aside disdainfully the conventional suffrage methods of propaganda. Ladylike these might

97

be, but they had no impact on the political world. She wanted results. Accordingly, in 1903, she formed the Women's Social and Political Union with the express object of putting pressure on political parties. Her methods of recruitment were lively. They included outdoor meetings and parades, both suffrage novelties. Her appeal in Manchester was largely to the intelligent working class, so far untouched by suffrage propaganda. By 1905, she was already in action. Sir Edward Grey, foreign minister in the new Liberal government, appeared in Manchester to develop and defend his party's policies. The WSPU sent a little working-class woman called Annie Kenney with Christabel Pankhurst to ask him what he intended to do for woman suffrage.

Sir Edward Grey made his speech, and questions were called for. The ladies stood up, but Grey made them no answer. He could hardly commit the Liberal party to suffrage, and he had no interest in it himself. On the other hand, a politician hates to say that he will do nothing. He passed the question over and replied to another. Annie Kenney unfurled a little cotton flag and stood up on her chair to ask again. Stewards rushed to haul her down. She struggled, and one of them stifled her remarks by holding his hat over her face. Christabel Pankhurst arose in her turn and repeated the question.

Sir Edward Grey still dodged the issue. The meeting was adjourned, and the audience was actually preparing to leave when the irrepressible Annie Kenney started again. This time she was actually struck and scratched. She and Christabel were seized by six stewards apiece and thrust into the street. Here they started a protest meeting as people came out, and they were arrested by the police for disorderly conduct. Resisting, they were roughly handled. No such riot involving respectable women had ever been witnessed in modern England.

Great was the sensation. None of the papers approved the heckling as such, but someone else's political party and the roughness of the police are familiar targets. In fact, such was the criticism that the Prime Minister thought it wise to give audience to a deputation of suffragists. He even admitted their arguments were unanswerable, but refused to do anything for them, sending them away with the advice to "go on pestering."

It was immediately clear to Emmeline Pankhurst that a very small amount of disorderly conduct had done more for the suffrage cause than years of peaceful propaganda. With the speed of a born general, she marshaled her forces and placed herself at their head. Ill treatment, if it could be provoked, would bring advantage. She herself had the heart of a lion and would stop at nothing.

In this way was born the English suffragette movement, whose characteristics were militancy and direct political action. Sensation was its lifeblood. It passed from awkward questions to awkward acts. Suffragettes paraded in front of 10 Downing Street. Removed by the police, they reappeared, chained to the railings. A woman threw herself in front of the King's horse as it was winning the Derby, perishing to make a sensation for woman suffrage. Eventually the suffragettes started vandalism, breaking windows, destroying mailboxes, setting fire to empty houses. Each outrage brought furious reaction, which provoked the suffragettes to something worse.

The government retaliated with arrests and imprisonment. These merely gave a scandalous publicity to the state of British prisons and the treatment of arrested persons by the police. Notwithstanding, sentences were made more severe. The suffragettes fought back by hunger-striking. The government, appalled, released its prisoners. They went back to their former tactics. Force-feeding was next resorted to, but the practice was not possible for long without killing the patient. The government finally took refuge in what was called the cat-and-mouse treatment, releasing prisoners when they seemed on the point of death, rearresting them to serve some more of their sentence when they recovered.

This war, for it was no less, started in 1905 and rose from one climax to another through the years before World War I. The bulk of British suffragists stood aloof from it, horrified. Yet

they, too, were galvanized by it. Open-air meetings and processions became part of their propaganda. Mrs. Pankhurst's
doctrine of political responsibility was everywhere discussed.
According to her, the party in power was at fault for not introducing suffrage. It was therefore the duty of every suffragist
to campaign against Liberals by every means in her power. If
Tories, when their turn came, refused the measure, they also
must be pulled down. This was hard to swallow for those who
had party convictions, but it contained a core of political
knowledge. Pressure gets things done. You must pull the right
lever if your efforts are not to be vain. In short, at the cost of
exacerbating tempers, the suffragettes made their cause a living
issue.

The first effect of this movement across the Atlantic was felt
through Harriot Stanton Blatch. In touch with the English suffrage groups through her mother, she had followed Mrs. Pankhurst's start. She saw in it several things which the American
suffrage movement must learn.

Most important of these was a direct connection with the
working women who would get most benefit from the passing
of suffrage law. So far the American suffragists had held aloof
from working-class leaders, notably from the emerging trade-
union movement. Early feminists had been outstanding women
concerned for the freedom of their own daughters and sisters.
The foreign-immigrant population was hardly regarded as a
citizen body, particularly since a great many women spoke no
English. Miss Anthony, ever liberal, had made some efforts to
draw in the working class. But with the whole nation to convert, even she had her hands full. Her successors had done little.
Mrs. Catt, a Midwesterner and well-to-do, had small understanding of the industrial poor. Dr. Shaw, for all her slum experience, never struck out a line of her own. It was left to
Harriot Blatch, her mother's true daughter, to tackle single-
handed a fresh problem.

In January 1907 she gathered a group of forty people on
Fourth Street in New York, just off the Bowery, to discuss how

Harriot Stanton Blatch speaking at a street corner.
(*Brown Brothers*)

to put fresh life into the movement. It was agreed that propaganda must become more dramatic, that working-class and
professional women must be drawn together and incorporated
into the movement, that its workers must forthwith become
politically minded. On these three principles the Women's
Political Union was founded. Harriot Blatch wasted no time in
getting into action. In the following month the New York
legislature was holding its perfunctory annual hearings on suffrage, which had not been acted upon for thirty years. Mrs.

Blatch took up to Albany a couple of trade-union women who
startled everyone by introducing a lively air into the tired
routine. She began to hold public meetings in New York and
to canvass the unions. Under her auspices, suffrage held its first
outdoor meetings in many years. League members were taught
to analyze potentialities of new recruits, and a card catalog of
members was set up by political districts. In a year and a half,
the Union was nineteen thousand strong. It had campaigned in
the local elections against assemblymen opposed to suffrage,
covered the polls with propaganda, paraded decorated autos,
set up a campaign in Albany to authorize woman poll-watchers.
In the summer of 1908, Mrs. Blatch led a trolley-car campaign
through New York State, starting from Seneca Falls and ending
at Poughkeepsie, with open-air meetings at every stopping point.
She began with seven speakers, but the pace was too hot for
five of them. She ended with only one helper, happy to carry
the banners and pass out literature, but never capable of speaking for more than five minutes at a time.

By the following spring, Mrs. Blatch was ready for the serious
political work. She had opened an office on East Twenty-
second Street in New York from which she ran a systematic
campaign to rouse the legislature. A catalog was begun, in-
dicating the suffrage standing of New York politicians. Those
unalterably opposed were to be defeated if possible in the pri-
maries. When chosen, they must be questioned and forced to
state their position. When the election actually came, Mrs.
Blatch had succeeded in placing five watchers at the polls who
proved their efficiency so well that the Volunteer Poll Watchers'
Association took up women. In the following year she made
another attack on the suffrage bill, which had not even been
mentioned on the floor of either house for fifteen years. She
petitioned for its discharge from the Judiciary Committee,
since the growth of the movement gave its proponents a right to
have a decision. Her motion was defeated. She took it up to the
Senate, where it was also defeated. But the result was that suffrage had been debated in both houses.

In the same year, 1910, she invited the National-American leaders to join New York suffrage forces in a really big Fifth Avenue parade. The New York State suffrage association expressed the opinion that such a demonstration would set back the suffrage cause for fifty years. Anna Shaw, too, expressed grave doubts about this radical proposal, but she consented to take part. There were a number of suffrage clubs in New York, including the College Equal Suffrage League, which produced two hundred women dressed in caps and gowns, carrying banners. The parade therefore went fairly well, considering the inexperience of its producers; but the chief suffrage leaders climbed into autos and merely whisked down the avenue "in one flash of yellow," the suffrage color. The Women's Political Union decided that future parades would contain no autos, that everyone must march the entire route. Furthermore, there would be preliminary instruction in walking. The annual suffrage parade in New York became a feature of the city's calendar, growing larger and more colorful on every occasion. Dr. Shaw, converted now, walked with the rest.

While this lively movement was developing in New York, Mrs. Catt, now a widow, came back from Europe. She had never lost touch with suffrage, having retained the presidency of the international suffrage organization which had been started under her auspices a few years earlier. Mrs. Catt was the last person likely to sympathize with Emmeline Pankhurst or to woo the trade unions as did Harriot Blatch. Nevertheless, the political and organizational aspects of the new movement interested her greatly. She was acute enough to perceive that unless the suffrage movement was invigorated from within, the influence of Mrs. Pankhurst would produce an extremist party in America. Already Mrs. Blatch had invited Mrs. Pankhurst from England, and in 1911 she actually came. By then Mrs. Catt had begun a counterrevolution.

After consulting with a number of New York leaders, she decided that the city of New York should provide an example of a vital suffrage organization. A Woman Suffrage Party was formed, taking in all suffrage groups. This divided the city (on the model of Tammany Hall) into sixty-three election districts and 2,127 precincts. Members of all suffrage clubs in the city were classified by precinct, and a great search commenced for 2,127 precinct captains and sixty-three district leaders, not to mention borough and county superintendents above these. Chief qualification was a willingness to work, week in and week out. District leaders gathered their own captains for training, and they set to work inside their precincts. Each was instructed to map her area, marking every church, factory, school, saloon, shop, settlement house, or other prominent building. In the light of what such surveys revealed, activities were planned. Meanwhile, the central organization opened a headquarters with separate departments for press, organization, literature, and political work. Bulletins were issued every day and press conferences held weekly. Tons of literature were distributed free.

A few days after Mrs. Pankhurst had spoken in Carnegie Hall, the Woman Suffrage Party held a meeting in the same spot with delegates and alternates from every assembly district. Some of these were wives and relatives of Tammany, and the aspect of this meeting made New York politicians look thoughtful. They could count suffrage strength in terms they understood, and it was formidable.

The Woman Suffrage Party organization was the first systematic attempt to muster suffrage forces for the conquest of a major city. It made an immediate sensation. Philadelphia, Chicago, and other great cities followed its example. Meanwhile, in New York the suffrage issue became present everywhere—at school meetings, church meetings, street meetings. Women began to appear at Tammany picnics, firemen's parades, Wall Street dinners. They handed out literature in the streets, made speeches, thought up stunts. Suffrage bazaars, balls, art exhibits raised money and were good propaganda. Suffrage buttons and calendars were sold. Posters in seven languages were put up.

The objectives of the Woman Suffrage Party were to convert politicians, to revive the state suffrage association, which had almost given up in despair, and to put direct pressure on Albany. Accordingly, after the election of 1910, suffrage leaders called on each assemblyman with a delegation from his own district. State senators were similarly visited. One man said he had canvassed his district and not five women in it wanted to vote. His district leader had 189 signatures from his own block in front of him next morning. Another who said there was no enthusiasm in his district was invited to an enormous district meeting.

The legislature resisted stoutly, refusing to bring up the amendment. In consequence, the second Fifth Avenue parade in 1911 was planned as a great protest. This time there was no hanging back. The women marched eight abreast, representing the trades, the professions, the arts, and the home. Flags and mottos came with them. Graduates walked in caps and gowns. Students had their own section. Old women rode. Mothers wheeled small children. Whole families walked in the procession together. The demonstration was followed by monster meetings, ten thousand gathering in Union Square alone.

Suffrage was on the march again. The state of Washington was won by Mrs. Emma De Voe, a product of Mrs. Catt's Organization Committee. California, after frantic efforts, was conquered at last. Ten thousand workers labored all over the state. Every village had its meeting. There were pennants, post cards, billboards, floats, streetcar advertisements, and suffrage buttons. Millions of pages of literature were given away.

This California victory encouraged the suffragists but really roused the opposition. Nor did California command many electoral votes. Far more significant were the referenda in 1912 of Michigan and Ohio. If woman suffrage could break out of the Far West and dominate two populous and powerful states, it would have to be taken into consideration by politicians.

Both sides girded themselves for the fray. The suffrage campaigns in both states were intense. Enthusiasm mounted. It was known that the antisuffrage forces would stop at nothing. Ballot-box stuffing, false counts, and illegal voting were to be expected. Saloonkeepers were hard at work, immigrants were being drilled on how to vote. There might be efforts made to introduce fraudulent ballots which did not print the suffrage amendment. Threats and bribery kept businessmen in line. All the same, it seemed so obvious that the general feeling ran in favor that the suffrage leaders had high hopes. Both states were lost. In Michigan, early returns were favorable, but a number of precincts held back their figures, giving no explanation. When these were released, they each had a suspiciously large majority against the motion. A tremendous uproar followed, and the governor accused the brewers of being parties to a fraud. The referendum was submitted again and defeated by a larger majority. But the increase in the total vote and in the adverse vote was identical to the last digit. Such frauds were possible only with the collusion of the bipartisan election officials, bought or controlled by secret orders. Meanwhile, in Ohio, liquor interests openly boasted that they had defeated the suffrage referendum. A few years later, an antisuffrage petition in Ohio came under scrutiny, and about ten thousand signatures were checked. Almost nine thousand of these proved fraudulent.

These Midwestern defeats were intensely disappointing, suggesting that fraud and bribery counted for more than the general will. Yet, inspired by the example of New York, suffrage agitation multiplied a hundredfold. By 1915, New York's efforts had actually brought about a referendum. The state swung into a campaign which made preceding efforts look small.

Mrs. Catt opened a school for campaign workers. Canvassing squads and gaily-decorated mobile headquarters descended on every town and postal district. On Mother's Day, clergymen were asked to preach a suffrage sermon. On the Fourth of July, the Women's Declaration of Independence was read from courthouse steps. On Labor Day, the Women's Trade Union League made suffrage speeches at workers' parties. In the fall, country markets and fairs had suffrage booths with speakers. Newspapers were published in twenty-six languages in New York State in those days. A publicity council handled propaganda in them all.

Meanwhile, in New York City, the pace grew dizzying. There were special suffrage days for barbers, street cleaners, bankers, railway workers, longshoremen, and many others. There were sandwich girls, theater and movie nights with speeches in the intermissions. Windows of vacant stores were hired for displays. There were suffrage restaurants. There were torchlight processions, street dances on the lower East Side; Irish, Syrian, Polish rallies. There were outdoor concerts and open-air services. Every district had its bonfire. There were balloons, tableaux, and Chinese lanterns. At the end of October, just before the election, there was a final parade up Fifth Avenue of women representing every county and city in the state. They started up the avenue at one. At six they were still marching, and the stenographers and nurses coming off duty joined the parade.

Tugboat hired by Woman Suffrage Party to deliver a suffrage torch to women of New Jersey. (*The Bettmann Archive*)

Banner carried in a New York parade (*Culver Pictures*)

Watchers finally went home to dinner, leaving the suffrage forces moving and singing.

Everything humanly possible had been done in New York, yet it was not enough. No political party supported the amendment, and it was lost. Suffrage had gained enormous ground, yet the task of fighting for forty-eight states under such conditions was endless.

The opposition, in its turn, was growing in power. Anti-suffrage women were becoming fashionable in snobbish circles.

These "Antis" did little harm, but they did give politicians a chance to say that women did not want suffrage. Besides, their enrollment from the upper crust indicated that big business in general was siding with liquor. As women had emerged into public life, they had nearly always been connected with schemes for social betterment. Thus manufacturers' associations and chambers of commerce regarded women as impractical idealists who, knowing nothing of business, would ruin prosperity by pampering the workers.

Meanwhile, ever since the 1880s, brewers had been organized to tax every barrel of beer for a defense fund. Hard liquor had followed suit. Theoretically this money, which by now amounted to very large sums, was to be expended in fighting prohibition. Actually woman suffrage was considered in some ways more dangerous because it was harder to repeal. A German-American association, ostensibly social, had been formed by the brewers to bind their interests together. Its money was active everywhere against suffrage. Its agents turned up in state after state at crucial moments. What they actually did could not often be proved, but they controlled through the saloons large blocs of votes and were active in organizing immigrant voters.

These forces converged on the state legislatures. It was often comparatively easy to kill a suffrage motion in committee by pressure on its members. If it came to a vote on the floor, legislators were bribed or threatened with ruin. Many a man who would not take money for himself felt bound to be influenced by a contribution to the party or the knowledge that those who asked a favor of him controlled blocs of voters. When the railroad, oil, and general manufacturing lobbies joined liquor in agitating against suffrage, it was easy to see how the issue could be put off year after year.

Even if suffrage did get a referendum, the prospects of the women were discouraging. Immigrants sold their votes or took their politics from the general mass of their own countrymen. The politically minded rank and file mainly voted the party ticket. Leaders, playing for patronage and graft, could not afford to be independent of those who contributed to campaign funds. They therefore resisted committing their party to suffrage. Under these conditions, it hardly seemed possible that women's enthusiasm could be kept at the present pitch. It was time to turn away from state campaigns and make a fresh attack on the federal amendment. Here too the inspiration came from England.

Of all the great suffrage leaders, Alice Paul is the youngest. She is characteristically a twentieth-century product. She had been, for one thing, through the educational mill as we understand it, and was just completing her PhD. Her field of interest, too, was social studies. Of good Quaker stock from Moorestown, New Jersey, Alice Paul is in many ways a modernized version of Susan Anthony. She too is a general, and she has the same complete forgetfulness of self. But Miss Anthony and the other leaders had to struggle for their independence and in consequence came to suffrage work late; Miss Paul's education had gone smoothly at the pace one would now expect. In 1912, she was in her middle twenties and had spent 1910–1911 in England, residing in various settlement houses and rounding out her studies by firsthand experience of British conditions.

She found the English slums appalling and, like Dr. Shaw in Boston, despaired of making an impression. Her attention was caught by Mrs. Pankhurst, now at the height of her notoriety. Here at least was a woman who would not sit down under injustice. Mrs. Pankhurst took action. Her followers, young and enthusiastic, were moving mountains in a visible way. The suffrage issue had become inescapable, and Mrs. Pankhurst's group had made it so. Alice Paul joined it, eager for the martyrdoms of jail and forcible feeding. She experienced both. She tasted the excitement as well as the unpleasantness, felt the companionship of a devoted band. But America was her country, and she did not remain to fight for British suffrage. She sailed for home, determined to wake up the suffrage movement when she got there.

Mrs. Pankhurst was both direct and politically minded. Miss

Paul, looking at problems the same way, perceived that a federal amendment was the shortest route. Since her emotions and energies were not tied up in state work, her thoughts turned naturally to Washington as Miss Anthony's had done long before.

After 1889, when the National and American associations had fused, state organizations, especially from the West, objected to coming all the way to Washington for the annual conventions. Miss Anthony was forced to consent to conventions elsewhere. It followed that pressure could no longer be put on Congress, now that national leaders did not regularly meet in Washington. As in the New York legislature, a congressional committee still held an annual hearing. But in 1912 there had been no favorable report in either house for twenty years and no report at all for the past sixteen. In 1910, Dr. Shaw had attempted to remedy this by a convention in Washington addressed by President Taft and the presentation of a petition with more than four hundred thousand signatures on it, including those of many distinguished people, not all women. The sole upshot had been a hopeless hearing before the Judiciary Committee of the House, determinedly hostile. Meanwhile, the victories of Washington and California inspired hope in the states. Unwilling to commence a prolonged siege of Congress, the National-American had poured its resources into state campaigns. Its representation in Washington had been entrusted to the wife of a congressman. Mrs. Kent had taken the job on the understanding that it did not involve any work. The National-American paid her ten dollars for her expenses in connection with the annual hearing. She returned them the change.

Alice Paul's first demonstration for Mrs. Pankhurst had found her one of a deputation of more than a hundred who attempted to enter the Houses of Parliament. They were arrested and detained in the policemen's billiard room at Cannon Row, which seems to have been the largest room in that station. Alice, who was wearing a small U.S. flag, sat on the billiard table and talked with a tall, red-headed girl who was wearing another. Her name was Lucy Burns; she came from Brooklyn and was a graduate of Vassar. She had been studying in Germany for the last two years, had recently arrived in England on vacation, and had been swept into the suffragette movement. The two American girls were several times arrested for holding demonstrations outside meetings held by Asquith, Lloyd George, Churchill, and other prominent Liberals campaigning for the general election of 1910. Their adventures in and out of jail cemented a firm friendship; after Lucy's return to America they decided to work for suffrage together. Encouraged by Jane Addams and permitted by Dr. Shaw, they descended on Washington to see what could be done about the amendment.

Alice Paul and Lucy Burns were another suffrage team, as faithful to each other as Susan Anthony and Mrs. Stanton. Lucy, large and highly colored, was a physical contrast to the dark and slender Alice Paul. She was equally devoted and equally courageous. In a crisis, her gaiety and resource were invaluable. Nevertheless, Alice Paul was unquestionably the leader. She had the more incisive mind, the greater sense of generalship, the larger capacity for work. It was not that Lucy Burns was deficient in these things, but that Alice Paul was a truly exceptional woman whose powers of command were felt by all who knew her. What was more, they were hardly ever resented because Alice worked harder and longer than anyone else, never demanding from others what she herself would not willingly do. She had no detachment, however. Her flashes of humor illuminated events but left fundamentals alone. Alice Paul saw things in her own way, and nothing would move her. In her single-minded fashion she advanced, as Miss Anthony had done, to capture Washington without resources.

8

The Crusade of Alice Paul
1912–1918

There were several suffrage clubs in Washington, but their activities were social. There was even supposed to be a suffrage headquarters—though this, without Dr. Shaw knowing it, had closed. Armed with its address and a list of suffrage supporters, many of whom had moved away, Alice Paul and Lucy Burns arrived at the end of 1912. They took a basement on F Street, a long, narrow room partitioned off at the back into small storerooms. Here they called a meeting in which Mrs. Kent introduced Miss Paul as her successor.

Those ladies who took the trouble to attend found a pale, slender woman with a quiet manner and an air of fragility which was deceptive. Miss Paul had been something of an athlete at Swarthmore, and her physique proved capable of bearing strain. Her dark mass of hair was gathered simply into a heavy knot on the nape of her neck. She had no pretensions to beauty, though her face was a regular oval, her cleft chin firm, her eyes gray and large. Except in moments of crisis, her whole expression was impassive, often withdrawn. Her voice was low and pleasant. She did not speak often, and seldom without a pause for consideration. But when she did speak, her powers of analysis were devastating. There seemed nothing left to be said.

Nothing was more remarkable about Alice Paul than her ability to get work out of people. She started at once on a round of calls. Two ladies she found at home together recalled somewhat later their startled looks at each other after their visitor had left. Neither had intended to do anything, but each had promised a monthly sum to the cause and regular hours of work. The secret seems to have been that Alice never begged.

She put requests tersely in the full expectation that they would be granted. "Mrs. Gardner, the trappings for the parade horses have been ruined. Will you order some more? They must be delivered tomorrow night!"

"Miss Ross, will you go to Wyoming on Saturday and organize a state convention there within three weeks?"

"Miss Younger, will you deliver the memorial address on Inez Milholland?"

Miss Younger, who by this time knew Alice Paul well, found strength to protest.

"I can't. I don't know how to do it."

"Oh," said Miss Paul, tossing the problem back, "just write something like the Gettysburg Address."

Miss Younger, though no Lincoln, delivered the speech. Miss Paul wasted no time on thanks. Her eye was on the future. She presented another challenge in the perfect confidence that it would be met. It usually was.

Within a short time, the basement in F Street was humming like a beehive. The situation in Washington, Miss Paul pointed out, could and should be altered. The movement was gaining ground in the nation. Two more states had granted full suffrage in 1912, making a total of eight. Thus the women voters and the men who had admitted them were a formidable force. How were these voters to be used? They could hardly migrate in a body to other states and agitate there. Yet to let them feel content with what they had won was sheer folly. The suffrage movement could not afford to lose an organization that had carried a state referendum. It must not come out poorer in resources as a result of each success. The voters in the suffrage states must put their pressure on Washington. With their help, a federal amendment was far more practicable than in the eighties.

To campaign state by state must put the victory off for untold years. After sixty years of agitation, only a few states had been won. None of them was populous or important. All were in the Far West. In the East and in the Midwest defeats had been endless. Some state constitutions had proved almost impossible to amend. The movement was still in its infancy throughout the South.

Only in Washington could the problem be solved on a national scale. Congress already contained friends of suffrage, both liberal politicians and delegates from suffrage states. These needed to be aroused by pressure from their home districts. An active lobby in Washington was also essential.

Along these lines the work on F Street developed with extraordinary speed. Miss Paul's organization had not only to establish an active lobby, but to arouse nationwide support. It had also to raise its own funds for the work. Its help, to be sure, was almost all unpaid. Women gave up social engagements. Office workers dropped in after hours and stayed sometimes till midnight. Even then the place was understaffed. Workers would go out on F Street and bring in women to help with the letters. In fact, busy shoppers began to find it wise to bypass F Street if they did not want to spend the rest of their day there.

One of the little back rooms in the F Street basement was Alice Paul's private office. Lights always burned in it late, sometimes till morning. Alice and Lucy sat up night after night to get through mountains of work they could not concentrate on earlier. By day, the telephones were constantly ringing. People had to be seen, the press interviewed, meetings attended, arrangements supervised, somebody discovered to do this or that. One woman remarked that she had worked with Miss Paul for three months before she ever saw her find time to take her hat off. For a while she lived in an unheated room, not for cheapness but to prevent her being tempted to sit up reading for pleasure. In the same Spartan way, she avoided a bookstore which was opened by a friend, lest she see something there and start to read it. What she did herself, she demanded unrelentingly from other people.

Early in 1913, Miss Paul was ready with her first big Washington demonstration. It was an interesting year with Woodrow Wilson assuming the presidency and a Democratic majority in

Congress. With a fine sense of publicity, Miss Paul timed her Washington parade for the day before the inauguration. Wilson, met at the station, looked around surprised.

"Where are the crowds?"

"Over on the Avenue watching the suffrage parade," was the answer.

They were indeed. On Pennsylvania Avenue, the parade had degenerated into a riot. Miss Paul had gathered more than five thousand women, a remarkable effort after a few months' work. But the crowd which had come in for the inauguration was far from friendly. The Democratic party had never given encouragement to suffrage, and the representatives of the South were particularly hostile. Miss Paul had obtained a police permit, but the parade was inadequately protected, the force having reserved its strength for the following day. The women almost had to fight their way and took an hour to pass the first ten blocks. At Sixth Street, the crowds on either side came so close together that three marchers could not walk abreast. Students of Maryland Agricultural College, coming to the rescue, formed a line on either side and attempted to break the crowd in front by sending on a vanguard with locked arms. But hooligans soon passed from obscene language to spitting on the women, slapping them in the face, throwing burning cigar stubs, and trying to trip them up. Fist fights broke out between the persecutors and the protectors. Troops had to be called up from Fort Knox to restore order.

During the outcry which followed, in which the chief of police lost his job, Miss Paul scanned the papers well content. The suffrage movement had been dramatically introduced to Wilson, and it was not long before she was able to ask him about his attitude toward the movement. He replied that the issue had never been brought to his attention. He would be glad to be further informed before he made up his mind. Miss Paul settled back to deprive him of this excuse to dodge the problem.

The new President called immediately for a special session of

Congress to deal with tariff problems. Miss Paul and thirty supporters visited him to tell him that suffrage was of all questions the most urgent. Within ten days, at Miss Paul's instigation, the College Equal Suffrage League and the National Council of Women Voters had both seen the President. Pushed hard in this way, he excused himself from action because the session was too busy. This did not save him from a huge demonstration on the day the session opened. Delegates from all congressional districts of the country brought petitions, held a mass meeting, and marched to the Capitol, where the suffrage amendment was formerly brought to the attention of both houses. The remarkable speed with which all this was organized little more than a month after the inauguration was a startling example of the efficiency of Alice Paul.

Meanwhile, these activities were by no means her only preoccupation. She was in the throes of organizing a nationwide Congressional Union. State associations, engrossed in their own affairs, had little time for Washington. The District of Columbia was multiplying lectures, tableaux, receptions, benefits, or outdoor meetings to raise money; yet it could not be expected to carry a national campaign unaided. Nor could a lobby succeed in Washington without constant pressure on congressmen from home. The Congressional Union, founded with the blessing of Dr. Shaw, was an associate member of the National-American on a par with state organizations or the New York movement of Harriot Blatch. It adopted purple, white, and gold as its special colors, the last two those of the National-American, but the purple associated with Mrs. Pankhurst. It sent workers into the field with a monster petition which was presented to the Senate in July in a procession of decorated autos.

Miss Paul took great pains with her fieldworkers. She did not much care how young they were, preferring enthusiastic girls in their teens to tired older women. She personally devoted several hours to each one before she took up her task. Her organizers were told to pay no attention to the state suffrage party, by no means always friendly to this intruder in their midst. Each should establish herself in a good hotel and make her headquarters either the lobby of the hotel or a shop window. She should visit the papers first thing, then call on women whose names had been supplied to her. These she must ask to serve on a committee to arrange a meeting. National headquarters would send out a speaker. The organizer next established a permanent group, always preferring a few active members to a number of idle ones. She then went on to the next town. Eventually she came back to Washington and made her report. Miss Paul sent her immediately to the Capitol to lobby there. She learned what was going on in Congress, while representatives were glad to talk with a girl who had been working in their own constituencies. A change of scene, said Miss Paul, kept people fresh.

In August of the same year, 1913, the National Council of Woman Voters held its annual convention in Washington and, urged on by Miss Paul, voted to concentrate on the federal amendment. Processions and deputations of all kinds were bringing pressure on Congress. Representatives were besieged by their own constituents as floods of mail poured in, elicited by the work of the Congressional Union. Miss Paul meanwhile was continuing the education of the President by sending him delegations from the women of New Jersey, women in industry, clubwomen, and Democratic women.

In November the Union found funds to start its own paper. It had spread out of the F Street basement onto the first floor and was making plans for further expansion. A new session of Congress was about to open. Miss Paul, whose deputation to the President on this occasion had failed to get an appointment, called up the White House. The deputation, she calmly informed a horrified official, was on its way. It would wait until the President either had leisure or flatly refused to see it. On arrival, it was admitted.

Two or three weeks later, the National-American converged on Washington for its annual convention and also desired to send a delegation, demanding that Wilson call on the Democratic party to act. The unfortunate President, who was

Suffrage parade on Pennsylvania Avenue in Washington in 1914. This is not the famous parade at which there was a riot, but notice how the enormous crowd is bursting into the roadway to get near the paraders. (*Brown Brothers*)

ill, excused himself. The delegation, headed by Dr. Shaw, insisted on staying in Washington until he recovered. Slightly battered by now, he told the women that he was the representative of the Democratic party, not its master. It was not for him to impose his own views upon it.

Congress still refused to act, though the Senate committee, yielding to pressure, had brought in a favorable report. Miss Paul, whose campaign was proceeding in a planned fashion which is descernible through the welter of events, decided calmly that the time for the next stage had come. Despite constant pressure, a Democratic Congress and President had failed to push the amendment. It was time for Democrats to learn that women voters were a body which could not be trifled with. Miss Paul made preparations for opposing Democratic candidates in the 1914 elections, especially in states which already had woman suffrage. Here, as she acutely pointed out, both parties were in favor. It was merely a matter of exchanging one set of congressional friends for another.

This policy soon aroused fierce opposition. Many women had party affiliations. Others questioned the wisdom of opposing a suffrage friend merely because he was a Democrat, while very likely his opponent was an "Anti." To fight the Democrats would give offense without really affecting the elections. The National-American leaders felt the Congressional Union was getting out of hand. Mrs. Catt, immersed in preparations for the great New York campaign of 1915, was prominent among those who wished it brought under control. It had no right to impose its policy on the parent organization. Miss Paul was using the name and notepaper of the national organization to build a union expressing her personal views.

Such differences soon produced a split. Again the movement was divided, and Miss Paul proceeded in her own way. To her, the 1914 election was a mere preliminary to the presidential election of 1916. By the time this came up, her organization was geared to greater efforts. She formed it into what became known as the Woman's Party, incorporating in it the WSPU of Harriot Blatch. She infused this party with an impatience to which Mrs. Blatch gave forcible expression when she told the President that she was now an elderly woman and that the time had gone by when she would stand on street corners and ask the vote from every Tom, Dick, and Harry. In addition, Miss Paul had solidified her position by an alliance with a great deal of money.

Mrs. O. H. P. Belmont, millionairess and social leader, had contributed largely to suffrage for some years. She was a dominating woman, impatient of opinions which clashed with her own, and fond of bustle. Such qualities found outlet in the Woman's Party, for whom her money made possible a new headquarters. Cameron House was just across Lafayette Square from the White House, whence its banners of purple, white, and gold were distinctly visible.

From this strategic spot Miss Paul continued to direct publicity stunts bringing pressure on Congress. In 1915 she arranged a motor pilgrimage from San Francisco to Washington carrying a suffrage petition eighteen thousand feet long and bearing half a million names. It was met in Washington by a cavalcade of women on horseback accompanied by great numbers of banners carried by women in long purple capes, gold collars, and white stoles. But neither the spectacle nor the constant appeals of Miss Paul to the President and members of Congress brought decisive action. The Anthony Amendment did come to a vote on the floor of each house, but lost by a considerable margin. The President had been pushed to the point of saying that he did believe in woman suffrage, if won state by state. He even voted for it in a New Jersey referendum, which was defeated.

The 1916 campaign brought cautious acknowledgment from both major parties that the woman suffrage issue would have to be reckoned with. Both put off the day by leaving the question to the states. Both presidential candidates made further concessions. Hughes, fortified by his reformist wing, endorsed the federal amendment. Wilson made an eloquent speech to the National-American convention, prophesying that the cause would one day prevail. Miss Paul dismissed his words as meaning nothing.

The Woman's Party accordingly campaigned in the suffrage states against both the Democrats and Wilson. He carried ten of them out of the twelve, but his majority was certainly reduced. The good the Woman's Party had done was hard to determine, but the ill-will it had raised was very obvious. To Miss Paul, this did not matter. Let the Democrats abuse the women. As practical politicians, they dared not ignore them.

The President showed no signs of pressing for action. It is fair to say that throughout 1916 the administration had other matters on its mind. It was all very well to put up Wilson for re-election with the slogan "He kept us out of war." World War I, now two years old, was increasingly involving the United States against its will. No man was more reluctant to commit his country to the struggle than President Wilson. But he could not help himself.

Be it for this reason or another, Wilson resisted the appeals of every sort of delegation with which Miss Paul contrived to harass him. She was not surprised or even angry. This was not her way. She merely decided to pass on to cruder forms of demonstration. She had advance information that the President's message to Congress in December 1916 contained no reference to suffrage. Accordingly, five of the Woman's Party appeared at the Capitol to obtain seats in the front of the gallery, right opposite the Speaker's desk. Mabel Vernon, who was in the middle, had a big yellow banner pinned under her skirt. She quietly got it ready and, at a prearranged moment in the speech, the ladies dropped it smartly over the balcony, holding onto the top end by five tapes. It queried boldly:

MR. PRESIDENT, WHAT WILL YOU DO FOR
WOMAN SUFFRAGE?

Everyone turned full round to look. The President glanced up, faltered a moment, and went on. A buzz of comment ran through his audience. Guards headed for the gallery, trying vainly to force their way through crowds of women who had purposely packed themselves onto the steps. One of the pages on the floor jumped for the banner, caught it by one corner, and pulled it down. While the President finished his speech, the Woman's Party was passing out mimeographed reports on the affair to the press.

Alice Paul sent the President another deputation and received another refusal, which she used to convince the world that his heart was not set on suffrage. She had decided that the time had come for further measures. Acordingly, from that convenient headquarters opposite the White House, twelve women emerged on January 10, 1917, four with lettered placards and eight with the purple, white, and gold banners of the party. Marching in single file across the square, six took up their stance at the East Gate and six at the West. A placard on either side of each gate was flanked by two banners. The picketing had begun.

Picketing the White House was in those days a new sport, and it attracted plenty of attention. Wilson himself as he came out for his afternoon drive ignored the women. Next day, however, he laughed genially. Thereafter he politely took off his hat as he went by. Other people, both workers and sight-seers, stopped to stare. On the whole, the consensus was not unfavorable, though the usual verdict was "Wait till the rain and the snow. They'll soon get tired of it."

The pickets did not get tired. They stood through the rain in slickers and rubber hats. In the cold, the janitor of Cameron House trundled over from headquarters a wheelbarrow full of hot bricks for the pickets to stand on. Friendly passers-by fetched coffee for them. Branches of the Party gave spats and heavy gloves. When the session began, the Party extended its pickets to both Houses. Alice Paul was ingenious with new ways to keep up public interest. There were special picket days for different states, a college day, a teachers' day, a labor day, and

A delegation from New York takes its turn at picketing the White House gates. The slickers are left open to display the suffrage sash, even in the rain. The pickets are standing on mats to protect their feet from the wet, cold pavement.
(*Harris and Ewing*)

Susan Anthony's birthday. The slogans varied, as did the numbers or the trappings. The routine remained. Women issued in solemn procession from Cameron House, crossed the square, and took up their stations.

Inauguration Day dawned cold, wet, and windy. When visitors got off the train at Washington during the preceding three days, they had found a banner at the station; girls were handing out invitations to a demonstration at the White House on Inauguration Day. *"Come in Thousands,"* posters said everywhere.

When the day arrived, the horrible weather demanded special measures, but none thought of calling off the demonstration. A raincoat company, hastily summoned to Cameron House, was doing an enormous trade in tarpaulin hats, coats, and rubbers. Soon the procession appeared, very nearly a thousand strong, each marcher bearing a banner, which she had to work hard to hold up against the wind. The gates of the White House were securely locked. Police from Washington and Baltimore patrolled the grounds. Guards protested that they had not been told to receive the resolutions which the women wished to present. Eventually they took the calling cards of the leaders, and the procession encircled the White House four times, each circuit a mile. A few fainted, but none fell out unless she had to. Such spectators as cared to brave the weather were impressed even more by the women's courage than by the spectacle. One of those who took part on this day was eighty-two years old.

Congress adjourned on March third and was recalled five weeks later in a special session to declare war on Germany. Alice Paul's Quaker blood was up. She did not believe in war and was not going to allow it to deflect her. Had not Susan Anthony laid aside suffrage work in the Civil War, and with what sad effect? Alice Paul made her stand quite clear in her suffrage paper. The Woman's Party would continue to work solely for suffrage. Those of its members who desired to engage in war work must do so as individuals, not as Party members. The pickets would continue.

This was bound to be an unpopular position. Most people felt that a domestic issue ought to take second place for the time being. Besides, the pickets of the White House were conspicuous. All sorts of distinguished foreigners, French, English, Russian, and the like, came to visit their new ally. It was embarrassing to have them find pickets at the White House gates. Wilson had emphasized the purity of American motives, his desire of no gain from the war, his hope of imposing a just peace. It was awkward when suffrage placards began to carry his own words, commenting that what he said abroad was contradicted by what he did at home. It was irritating when foreign delegates waved approval.

By June the crowds who paused to stare at the pickets had become unfriendly. War hysteria was mounting, fed by propaganda and by acts of German sabotage, real or imagined. The pickets were attacked by some boys. One day a woman tore down a banner. It was the time of the evening rush hour, and the pavement was crowded with government·workers. Almost imediately a mob of them charged the pickets at both gates and destroyed their banners.

Four women courageously emerged from headquarters across the square carrying fresh banners. The crowd, impressed by their determination, fell back. At this the police, who had hitherto done nothing, intervened to protect the new pickets and escorted them to their stations.

Nothing more occurred that day, but the authorities had been alarmed. They could hardly allow constant riots at the White House gates. Besides, the crowds around the pickets might prove dangerous to the President's safety. His carriage might be held up. How easy for a treacherous German-American to get next to him then and fire a pistol! It was put to Alice Paul through a friendly mediator that the picketing must stop.

Could she explain why to the public, Miss Paul inquired.

"Oh, no!" One dared not put ideas into the enemy's head.

"The picketing," retorted Alice Paul, "will go on as usual."

The chief of police for the District was next to try his luck.

He warned Miss Paul that if the pickets went out again, they would be arrested.

She failed to see why picketing which had been legal in January had become less so in June. Her lawyers had advised her it was permissible. "The picketing will go on as usual."

Promptly the next morning Miss Paul telephoned police headquarters to say that pickets were going out. Rows of policemen stood outside Cameron House waiting to stop them. Ladies went calmly in and out, minding their own business; but no banners emerged. Presently Mabel Vernon came out with a box under her arm. She sat down on a bench in the middle of the square. Lucy Burns emerged and walked down the street. Katherine Morey strolled out in a different direction. While the police still had their eyes on the front of Cameron House, the three ladies met before the East Gate, opened Mabel Vernon's box, and pulled out a banner. They set it up and enjoyed several minutes of quiet before one of the policemen happened to turn and catch sight of it.

"The litle devils!" he exclaimed. "Can you beat that?"

The banner contained a simple quotation from the President's own words without any comment. The police were in a quandary. One of them started to make the arrest. Another protested:

"My God, man, you can't arrest that. Them's the President's own words!"

Only after several minutes of indecision did they take the ladies to the police station, where Lucy Burns demanded what was the charge.

"Charge! Charge!" a harassed policeman said. "We don't know what the charge is yet. We'll telephone you that later."

The charge was dropped, but the challenge of the pickets could not be allowed to pass. In the next few days twenty-five pickets were arrested. The last six of these were brought to trial on a charge of obstructing the highway and convicted, despite a spirited defense by Mabel Vernon, who brought to court suffrage photographs of the arrest at a time in the morning when the pavement was almost totally clear. The women were fined twenty-five dollars with the alternative of three days in the District jail if they refused to pay it. They went to jail.

The example of these first martyrs was rapidly followed by others. Three days in the District jail merely sufficed to acquaint the pickets with conditions to which they gave a wide publicity. The jail was filthy and infested with vermin and rats. One woman beat three rats off her bed in a single night. Other women complained that they could hear the rats shuffling the light chairs in the cells as they moved in the dark. The women's spirits were undaunted, however, and picketing continued.

Sentences soon mounted to thirty days and thence to sixty. The prisoners were transferred from the District jail to Occoquam Workhouse. This may have been done because of the outcry the newspapers were making. Some of the ladies had influential husbands who voiced their indignation at their treatment. However, the general police view appears to have been that a little acquaintance with harsh realities would soon work wonders. Occoquam turned out to be a change for the worse. Though prettily situated in rolling country with large and well-kept grounds and dairy cows, Occoquam also was filthy inside. The prison blankets were washed once a year, and such was their condition that matrons were warned not to touch them and were actually issued rubber gloves to protect their hands. A new inmate was given one clean sheet, the other being left on the bed from the previous occupant. Women with all sorts of diseases slept in the same ward, shared the same piece of soap. The beans, cereal, and soup which were their chief food all had worms. The suffragists made a game of counting these until one woman got fifteen at a single meal, when they lacked spirit to continue the count. No butter, sugar, or milk were provided except by doctor's orders. The milk from the dairy attached to the place was sold.

The suffragists did what they were told, but the workhouse authorities soon learned to dislike them. They collected a set of worms on a spoon and sent them to the superintendent. They were always bothering him with demands. They had brought toothbrushes with them which had been impounded with the rest of their things. They wished them issued at once. Where were their combs? They wanted to see their counsel. Were workhouse regulations according to law in the District of Columbia? Whittaker, the superintendent, became aware of their nuisance value. He ran the place his way, and they interfered.

Meanwhile, the police appeared to have given up. After nearly a month of arrests, picketing was allowed to go on as before. The crowds increased and were by no means friendly, while the inscriptions on the banners had become provocative. The Russian Revolution had begun, and the new Russian republic which was trying to form itself had granted votes to women. If the most reactionary nation in the world could pass such a measure, how could the President or the Congress of the United States delay? In the middle of August, the suffragists set up a new banner, addressing the President by the then-insulting title of *Kaiser Wilson*.

It had not been displayed more than half an hour before the mob was on the pickets. Banners were torn down after scuffles with their bearers. These returned steadfastly to Cameron House and came out with others. Such a movement merely attracted attention to suffrage headquarters, which was soon set upon by an angry crowd directed by a sailor. The front door was hastily locked, but someone produced a ladder, and the leader climbed up to pull down the suffrage banner which hung from a balcony over the door. Lucy Burns appeared from inside the house with a new suffrage flag. A friend followed her with a fresh version of the Kaiser Wilson proclamation. The two young women stood motionless on the balcony, holding their flags, while the crowd beneath them began to throw apples, eggs, and tomatoes. Someone fired a revolver. Luckily the bullet went through a window and lodged in a ceiling, narrowly missing two women standing inside. Three sailors now ran up ladders to wrestle with the women on the balcony for the flags.

Lucy Burns, who was heftily built, held on until the watchers thought she was going to be dragged over.

Two suffragists, meanwhile, got out of the back door and made their way to the White House gates, where they unfurled their banners and stood for fifteen minutes watching the struggle going on across the square. Police stood beside them, but made no move to quell the riot. Nor did they interfere when the sailor who had led the original tumult caught sight of the fresh pickets and charged. A policeman, watching the crowd before Cameron House, was asked by somebody, "Why don't you arrest those men?"

"Those are not our orders," the policeman said.

Two days later, police instructions had been changed again. The police themselves charged the pickets and handled them roughly, except in the rush hour, when they allowed the crowds to go to work.

The suffragists retaliated by concealing their banners in bags, newspapers, hats, or under their skirts. When they displayed them, the police would attack. Having captured the banners by main force, they would fall back. Immediately suffrage women, mingling with the crowd, would hand them fresh banners; and the job would have to be done again. On one occasion, eight pickets managed to display fifty-six banners in this fashion. The police chief was driven to visit Miss Paul again and warn her that she must call off the picketing.

"The picketing will go on as usual," answered Miss Paul.

She had little to lose and much to gain. The unpopularity of the Woman's Party throughout the country at large was great, it is true. But the police showed up at least equally badly, as did the scandalous conditions in jail. Meanwhile, the Congress and the country at large, finding headlines about suffrage steadily competing with the war news, were beginning to feel that something ought to be done. After all, there was a great demand for the amendment. There must be. Everybody was determined not to be bullied by that dreadful Woman's Party, but nevertheless . . . Miss Paul continued to send her pickets

out. Arrests started again. Another batch was shipped to Occoquam Workhouse.

Superintendent Whittaker was away at a conference of district commissioners at the White House. What was said there
was never known, but the superintendent was getting angry.
The attitude of his prisoners was increasingly defiant. They were
demanding to wear their own clothes and be treated as political
prisoners. Whittaker came back to his workhouse determined
to teach the women a lesson.

The newcomers, meanwhile, had been led to the admissions

Lucy Burns in jail. She is posing for the photographer in front
of her cell, whose furniture can dimly be seen through the
bars. This is an unflattering picture of Lucy, who is very naturally not looking her best. (*Harris and Ewing*)

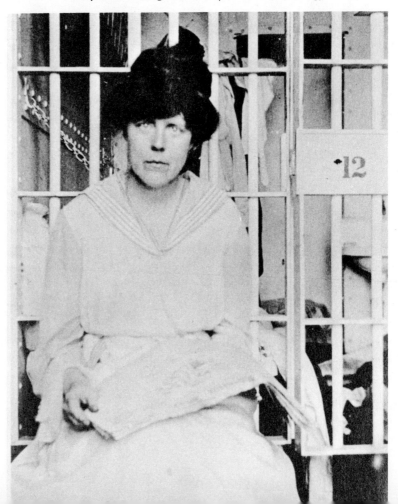

desk and asked the usual questions. They refused to answer and demanded to talk to the superintendent. They were told he was out and they would have to wait all night. They sat or lay down on the floor and prepared to do so.

Hours passed, and some male guards drifted in, a few at a time. The admitting officer, visibly nervous, made another effort at the questions. It was unavailing.

Suddenly the door burst open and the superintendent came rushing in, followed by more guards. The leader stood up and began to voice her demand.

"You shut up! I have men here glad to handle you," said Whittaker. "Seize her!"

Two men obeyed his orders, and the others pounced on the rest. Old Mrs. Nolan, over seventy and lame, was dragged across a courtyard in the dark, and down a corridor, where she was roughly thrown into a cell, landing on the bed. A companion, thrust in a moment later, hit the wall. The head of a third struck the iron bedstead, and she fell unconscious. Other women had been more violently handled. One had her body brought down twice over the back of an iron bench. Lucy Burns began to call the roll to find out if all were present. She was told to shut up. When she continued, guards handcuffed her and fastened her arms above her head in a position in which she remained all night.

The women found themselves in windowless cells, at once stuffy and cold, each furnished with a single bed and a mattress on the floor, all filthy. An open toilet in each was flushed by the guard, if he could be got to do it, which was not often. Next morning they were taken before the superintendent, having neither washed nor eaten since the preceding noon. Once more they claimed their rights and announced their intention of going on a hunger strike until these were granted.

Superintendent Whittaker was soon deep in trouble. The women's sentences had varied from six days for old Mrs. Nolan to six months for Lucy Burns. It was therefore impossible to prevent the story from getting to the papers. One of Mrs. Nolan's cellmates had suffered a heart attack and had been desperately ill all night, but the guards on duty had paid no attention. The other, hit on the head, had been long unconscious and was at first thought to be dead. Counsel for the women challenged their' commitment to the workhouse and demanded that they be brought back to court, where their condition shocked everyone. They were soon recommitted to the District jail, where they resumed their hunger strike.

Alice Paul herself was not the sort of leader who hung back. It chanced, however, that in the early summer she had been ill; while later she was too busy to waste her time in jail. It was not until Congress adjourned that she found time to join the pickets, taking with her a stenographer so as to lose no moment. She was sentenced to seven months and, arriving at the District jail, looked around her. The building in which she found herself contained about seventy-five women prisoners locked in three tiers of windowless cells whose gratings gave on the entrance hall. Ten suffragists who were inside appealed to her to ask for fresh air. Alice Paul'looked up and saw a high window with a rope hanging from it. She asked the matron why it was not opened. If they did let in a draft, they would have to give the colored prisoners more clothes, the matron answered.

Miss Paul wasted no more words, but opened the window. Guards wrested the rope from her hands and carried her to her cell. They set her down. Alice Paul had in her pocket a little volume of Browning. Instantly she drew it forth and launched it at the window. With her usual efficiency, she scored a bull's-eye, breaking the pane. By the time the last suffragist left jail, it had not been repaired, and ventilation was startlingly improved.

She went on a hunger strike at once, was forcibly fed, and soon became so weak that she had to be taken to the prison hospital. Mental specialists visited her to establish that she had a persecution complex and had fixed on the President as her personal enemy. They soon discovered Miss Paul was aggressively sane and entirely free from resentment. Notwithstanding, she was removed to a psychopathic ward, where a nurse was instructed to keep her under observation by flashing a light in her face every hour all night long. The hunger strike and forcible feeding continued.

The reports of the suffragists had been spread all over the country. Protests came raining in. The scenes at Occoquam had disgusted everybody. Miss Burns, Miss Paul, and several others were soon thought likely to die. Meanwhile, the Woman's Party was as active as ever. People were actually coming from considerable distances to take their turn at picketing and jail. Women's Party speakers were touring the country, addressing large audiences. Money was flowing into the party coffers. In fact, the picketing, which of itself had chiefly earned disapproval, had become popular through the martyrdom of the pickets. It was time for the government to pull its hand out of the hornets' nest.

The atmosphere in Congress was changing fast. The work of the Woman's Party was more than being matched by that of the National-American, aroused at last to seek a national amendment. Badgered on all sides, political powers were giving way. Even the opposition had other things on its mind. Temperance propaganda had brought a national prohibition amendment into the field of practical politics. Liquor interests had their own backs to the wall, and their attention was naturally distracted from woman suffrage. What point was there, meanwhile, in fighting the Woman's Party as long as the government was changing its mind?

Considerations such as these induced the government to give way all along the line. On December 3, 1917, the imprisoned pickets, even including Miss Burns and Miss Paul, were forthwith released. The House set January tenth for a vote on the suffrage amendment, and the President came out for it himself. This was victory indeed. All that remained was to get the votes, two-thirds of the Senate and two-thirds of the House, together with thirty-six states to ratify the amendment. The Woman's Party called a great mass meeting in which it presented prison pins to those who had served sentence. There need be no more martyrs. Suffrage again was on the march with victory in sight.

9

The Campaign of Carrie Catt
1915–1918

Dissatisfaction with the leadership of Dr. Shaw first showed itself in 1910 in resignations from the national board. Suffrage
appeared to be going nowhere. No states had been won since
1896. Indeed, the more favorable public opinion became and
the more numerous pledges were from politicians, the less likelihood there was of carrying a state. The forces of opposition,
tightly organized against increasing demand, appeared all-
powerful. Dr. Shaw, an individualist in Miss Anthony's old
style, had no political intuition. The new situation called for
countermeasures which she could not envisage or apply.

In spite of frustrations, however, the movement was really
advancing. The great resurrection in New York had begun.
The imaginative campaign that won California was soon to
follow. Other Western states were gained in the next few years.
Under pressure from the Congressional Union, the Anthony
Amendment was voted on in both Houses of Congress in 1914.

None of these signs of vigor was directed or called forth
by the national board. A New York headquarters was opened
in 1910, thanks mainly to the munificence of Mrs. Belmont.
The officers of the board, however, remained widely scattered
and had other demands on their time. They seemed incapable of
sustained effort. In 1910, as we have seen, Dr. Shaw was able to
start what might have been a drive for the amendment by getting President Taft to address the national convention. The
effort was not followed up, and two years later no work was
being done in Washington. The arrival of Miss Paul produced
an organization permitted rather than inspired by headquarters.
When the Congressional Union broke away, Dr. Shaw was

blamed for letting it get out of hand. Its vigor after the split contrasted sadly with the helplessness of the parent organization.

By 1915 morale was lower than ever. The new vitality had been a product of state organizations undirected from above. Dr. Shaw was being buffeted by claims and counterclaims that her authority was no longer sufficient to resolve. The bulk of national money was raised in the East, yet much of it was being spent in the West to win small states with little influence on the nation. Meanwhile, suffrage had suffered a series of defeats in the Midwest; 1915 saw defeat in the East, where the failure of the huge New York campaign was underlined by other failures in Pennsylvania, Massachusetts, and New Jersey. Suffrage leaders, deeply discouraged, were ready for a squabble. Where ought the funds and efforts to be directed?

By the end of 1915 it was clear that Dr. Shaw must go. The National-American did not lack a pretext for her retirement. She was nearly seventy. She was, however, still vigorous and in full command of her faculties. The fire of her unmatched eloquence burned as brightly as ever. Demotion was a bitter blow to her, but she was above pettiness. If the movement could use her in another way, it was welcome to do so.

Equally strong was the demand for Mrs. Catt. She was now fifty-five and inclined to take the view that a younger woman was needed. But the reputation of her past years as president had been growing, while her recent activities in New York had demonstrated that she really was the ablest woman in the movement. Besides, the old argument still had weight. Her comfortable income allowed her to concentrate entirely on suffrage. Furthermore, Mrs. Frank Leslie had recently left her two million dollars to spend for the cause. The estate, to be sure, was tied up by litigation; but the very prospect of such a sum gave Mrs. Catt a position of exceptional power. It amounted to a sizable endowment of the movement.

Yielding to pressure from all sides, Mrs. Catt once more became national president. A different atmosphere was felt at once.

Mrs. Catt (*left*) and Dr. Shaw campaigning for suffrage.
(*Brown Brothers*)

She insisted on a working board composed of ladies of independent means like herself. Poor people could not give their whole time to unpaid work. Gratitude or affection never induced Mrs. Catt to retain a lieutenant who was hampered by poor health, finance, or family worries. She wanted their full time and gave her own.

National action, as she clearly saw, ought to concentrate on the federal amendment. This could not be left to the Congressional Union operating on a policy of its own. Miss Paul's political sense had led her to perceive that politicians will yield to certain sorts of pressure. Mrs. Catt's informed her that they could, if pursued intelligently, be won over. One of her earliest moves was to appoint a Washington Committee to assess feeling there and to make friends.

By 1916, a truly significant event had greatly improved the political prospects of suffrage. A number of states through the years had granted voting rights to women in municipal elections, for school boards, on tax and temperance questions. In general these had proved rather more a hindrance to full suffrage than otherwise. Women, content with voting on local issues, slackened effort. Politicians, able to estimate what proportion of women would vote with each party, lacked the stimulus which hope of attracting fresh votes might otherwise provide. The opposition was roused to greater activity by feeling the influence of women on the Temperance vote. Partial suffrages, however, had one attraction: they could be conferred by legislatures without a statewide referendum. In 1914, the state of Illinois, following this procedure, gave women the right to vote for presidential electors, or in other words to vote for President.

Hitherto the electoral votes of the suffrage states had been inconsiderable. Illinois was the first large state to give presidential suffrage, and the first state outside the Far West. It now became possible that women electors might cast the deciding vote for the next President. Accordingly Mrs. Catt led a national drive to get both parties to adopt a suffrage plank in their election platforms.

The Republican Convention of 1916 took place in Chicago. Mrs. Catt, who never made a move without careful preparation, had already caused her Congressional Committee to draw up appropriate planks for the two parties and submit them to friendly Republicans or Democrats in Congress. These had then been sent to the leaders of the conventions. All delegates had

received three letters about them. Presidential candidates had
been interviewed. In the individual states, suffrage deputations
had called on party leaders and had received many promises of
support. Newspapers had been canvassed, and many had come
out in favor. Resolutions by various state associations had been
procured. Women delegates, of whom there were a good many,
had been specially approached. As a culmination of all these
efforts, Mrs. Catt had planned a parade of twenty-five thousand
women through Chicago to the hall where the Convention was
in session.

The day dawned in torrents of rain. Every raincoat in the city
was hastily bought up for the paraders, while two poor elephants
who were to lead the way were draped with ponchos. A fireman's
parade on the same day was called off, but the suffrage forces,
though in greatly depleted strength, struggled gallantly through
the wet, eliciting a tribute to their determination from all who
saw them. They arrived at the convention hall at the very
moment when the Resolutions Committee was listening to the
women "Antis." One of these had just finished saying "Women
do not want the vote" when the doors opened and the wet mass
of the parade came pouring in.

The Republicans were in a quandary. Opposition from the
business interests of the East was strong. At midnight on the
preceding day, after a long session, the subcommittee on woman
suffrage had rejected the plank. Mrs. Catt's political committee
of Republican women was untiringly watching events. It presented a unanimous appeal from the women delegates. The
Resolutions Committee as a whole now reversed its subcommittee's verdict, adopting the resolution. Absentees at once demanded the vote be reconsidered. After much negotiation a
compromise was reached. The Republican party went on record
as favoring the extension of woman suffrage, but decided that
this ought to be done by the states. Having thus absolved themselves from taking action, the politicians went on to other
matters.

Although a defeat, this was at least a new departure in that neither major party had recommended suffrage in any way before. Mrs. Catt and her supporters went on to St. Louis, where the Democrats were holding their convention. Here they staged a "golden lane" of six thousand women dressed in white with yellow sashes and yellow parasols lining both sides of the street from the Jefferson Hotel, where the leaders were staying, down to the Colosseum, where they met. In spite of ill-feeling caused by the Woman's Party, the subcommittee reported in favor. When its leader stood up to say so, the gallery appeared to rise as one, cheering, waving flags, and opening the golden parasols. But when the roll call for the voting began, all died away into sudden silence, and a rustle of paper on which women were noting down the names of their opponents was heard ominously.

Even so, the Democratic Convention would not do more than the Republican one. It favored suffrage, but left action to the states. The Democratic party had its own inner struggle on the subject. Its southern members still looked on suffrage as a northern cause, connected in the past with antislavery and forming part of the changes with which the North was still attempting to reconstruct the South. Then too, the activities of Miss Paul had infuriated Democratic politicians. In these circumstances, the Convention saw no reason to do more than the Republicans, though there was every argument for not doing less.

Half an hour after the close of the Democratic Convention, Mrs. Catt called a meeting of her national board. She announced a drive by her new Congressional Committee to test the effect on Washington of the cautious approval of both parties. In the meantime she asked for an emergency convention in Atlantic City in the fall. This being agreed on, she briskly dispatched a questionnaire to state presidents, asking what work had been done in the past six months and what was planned. She enclosed with it a list of subjects they should be prepared to discuss at Atlantic City. Next she went to see President Wilson, armed with reports on crooked dealings of the opposition in various referenda. She also called to his attention the provisions in some state constitutions which made amendments almost impossible. Her facts were impressive, as always; but Wilson would not declare for a national amendment. He consented, however, to address the Atlantic City convention and did so in the eloquent words which Miss Paul so disdained: "I come not to fight for you, but with you."

The real business of the Atlantic City convention, however, was revealed in secret session when Mrs. Catt unveiled what she called "The Winning Plan." If the right measures were taken and the right sacrifices made, she believed it possible to get a federal amendment passed in the next five years.

The suggestion had an electric effect. It was never Mrs. Catt's habit to put forward vague hopes as though they were plans. It would be necessary, she pointed out, to marshal all state forces under the command of the national board for the purpose of getting the amendment. This did not mean that state work should cease. On the contrary, the only true method of putting pressure on congressmen was winning successes in their home states. Mrs. Catt wanted not less state activity, but more. It must, however, be coordinated. She wanted it to burst out everywhere at the same time so that the opposition would not know where to counter it. Those states which had suffrage should concentrate on putting through their legislatures resolutions asking Congress to pass a federal amendment. States in which a referendum was impossible to obtain should press for what could be given by their state legislatures. In particular, those which already had municipal suffrage should campaign for the presidential vote on the model of Illinois. Other states, headed by New York, would meanwhile try once more for a referendum. Every victory would add momentum to the concerted drive.

Success would depend on secrecy and speed. No word of the plan must get out. State representatives were asked to sign a contract pledging their resources and promising to do their part. They agreed with enthusiasm. A fund of a million dollars would be needed. Eight hundred thousand was promised in twenty minutes. Two hundred full-time organizers were to be employed by the national movement. The national board was to set up a press bureau, a speakers' bureau, a publicity council, a committee for propaganda in foreign languages. A new national headquarters was planned in New York with part of the money Mrs. Catt obtained from the Leslie estate.

This was imaginative planning at last. Victory within five years! It would take the efforts of all, warned Mrs. Catt. There was no time for disputes and jealousies or personal feelings. The leaders of every state rose enthusiastically to meet the demand. Even the southerners with their insistence on states' rights were partly willing to agree.

There were now two centers to the movement. New York headquarters directed and controlled the efforts of the states, assisting them by organizers, leaflets, funds, or advice. The Congressional Committee, which had its own Suffrage House in Washington, focused pressure from everywhere on Congress. This meant that there were now two suffrage lobbies in Washington, that directed by Miss Paul which kept up pressure on its friends as well as its foes, and that of the national organization, equally systematic, equally devoted, but much larger.

The techniques of the two lobbies were similar. The purpose of their work was to direct the efforts of the friends they had and to make new ones. A good deal of a lobbyist's time was spent in visiting the offices of congressmen, either to ask advice or to call attention to facts which might otherwise have escaped notice. The pains taken by suffrage lobbyists may provide an instance of the devoted labors which brought about a national amendment.

The Congressional Committee sent out its callers in twos, partly because congressmen were nervous meeting single ladies, partly because a verbal admission made to two had more significance. All were carefully briefed. A congressman was a busy man, and the most eloquent presentation of a case would arouse his resentment if it took up too much of his time. He was also human and liked to talk as well as to listen. Interviews were

generally conducted by one woman, while her companion confined herself to an occasional sentence, lest between them they
take the ball away from their victim. If a congressman was unfriendly or rude, it was of the utmost importance never to argue
with him. People like to be right, and repartee arouses resentment. Never should anyone be given an opportunity of saying
flatly that he was against the national amendment. Once a man
had gone on record in this fashion, he was far less likely than
before to change his mind.

The interview should be brought to an end before the congressman found it necessary to break it off. After they left,
women should refrain from the slightest discussion of what had
been said, either in the corridors, where transoms were often
open, or in elevators, entrance halls, streets, or buses. Instead,
they should immediately retire to the nearest ladies' room and
write down notes, being careful that no passer-by, attendant, or
lobbying "Anti" saw them at it. These notes would form the
basis of a written report. This would be added to the congressman's special file—which already contained his personal and political history, his family and business connections, his friends,
his hobbies, his prejudices, tastes, and weaknesses. No information about a man was ever irrelevant to the purpose of winning
his vote. This file had naturally been studied by the interviewers
before they came to see him at all. They had also learned the
name of his secretary, whose influence and help could be decisive.

The business of a lobbyist was not primarily to convert her
congressman. Votes are not so easily won. It was rather to check
on the state reports about his attitude. It was also to keep up
the pressure by making him aware of a large and growing force
of public opinion. Most of the interviewing was done by suffragists who came to Washington for a month or so at a time.
The permanent staff, many of whose members lived at Suffrage
House during the session, was a committee of fourteen headed
by Maud Wood Park, one of Mrs. Catt's ablest lieutenants.
These communicated with state congressional chairmen. If let-

ters were needed from a man's constituents, if articles were required to appear in his hometown paper, the state chairmen, assisted by congressional aides, performed this job.

The efforts of the states called for by the Catt plan could not get going much before the beginning of 1917. In April of that year, America entered World War I. The suffrage movement as a whole was faced with the situation that Miss Paul, as we have seen, decided to ignore.

Mrs. Catt, as was usual on a question of tactics, took a view different from Miss Paul's. Women, she perceived, would enter war work whether suffragists did so or not. If the movement held back, it would not be in a position to press for its reward from a grateful country when victory was won. It was vitally important that suffrage and suffrage leaders take a prominent part in the mobilization of women. But not for this reason was she willing to postpone the Catt plan or to give up working for suffrage. "We must do both," she told the association. Each task was as important as the other.

Mrs. Catt lengthened her day in order to work on the Women's Committee of the Council of National Defense, of which Dr. Shaw became the chairman. At the same time she assumed the lead in starting war work by the suffrage movement as such. She soon had six departments concerned with food conservation, child welfare, women in industry, overseas hospitals, land army, and Americanization, all of which did useful work. Meanwhile, she was deep in a conference for state congressional chairmen, calling for extension of their suffrage work through county chairmen.

Thus urged by their versatile leader, the suffrage movement responded with enthusiasm. By the end of 1917, presidential suffrage had been granted by six state legislatures, including Rhode Island, first in the East. Meanwhile, all the equal-suffrage states had sent resolutions to Congress calling for a federal amendment. But these successes paled beside the November victory in New York. The New York referendum campaign had been, perforce, conducted in a far quieter way than the great effort of 1915. In wartime it seemed more suitable to concentrate on meetings, which were constantly held in every place, in every group, on every occasion. But the deciding thing came two weeks before the election. Tammany Hall said "Hands off the amendment!" This permission to go ahead had been wrung from Tammany by ceaseless propaganda practiced in New York. So many of the wives and daughters of New York politicians had been drawn into the suffrage movement that their lords and masters could resist no longer. Eroded from within, Tammany gave its permission. The result was a defeat in upstate New York, which was more than compensated for by the favorable returns in New York City.

New York was won for suffrage—the most populous state in the Union and a bulwark of those eastern states whose wishes still swayed the nation. The suffrage lobby hardly needed to underline the significance of this success. Politicians were looking on suffrage at last as something urgent.

While these successes were piling up in the country at large, the task of the Washington lobby had not been an easy one. In April 1917 Congress had made an agreement that no measures unconnected with war save necessary financial bills should be taken up that session. Looking around for some means to give effect to her growing influence in congressional terms, Mrs. Park decided to press the House for a rules change, which would not come under the heading of a bill. The Judiciary Committee, which had had suffrage under its wing for many years, was unalterably hostile. No report had been made to the House, and none was likely to be made. In fact, the great difficulty with the House was to get a bill debated on the floor. A woman suffrage committee would facilitate this, while the floor vote on its creation would demonstrate the growing strength of woman suffrage in Congress.

The committee was established, and as a result it became possible when Congress reconvened in November to press for consideration of a bill. The New York delegation of forty-three members was already changing sides. The number of electoral votes for President in which women had a share had risen to two hundred fifteen. The ball was rolling.

This situation, as we have seen, caused the government to call an armistice with Miss Paul, whose cohorts had been skirmishing away through 1917. All prisoners were released, and it was understood that the amendment would be voted on in the House and shortly thereafter in the Senate. The Woman's Party, decorating its martyrs with prison pins, took full credit for the victory. Meanwhile, Mrs. Catt, Mrs. Park, and all other leaders of the National-American announced with one voice that the Woman's Party had been nothing more than a hindrance and a nuisance.

There is something to be said for each view. Miss Paul's activities had certainly aroused politicians to fury. Patient lobbyists had listened to many a tirade from an outraged congressman, venting his feelings on the nearest suffragist at hand. Mrs. Catt had thought it necessary to proclaim that the national movement had no connection whatsoever with the pickets. Besides, when the Woman's Party did lobby, its immediate object was often different from Mrs. Park's, causing endless confusion among congressional supporters. In view of the Catt plan and the impressive victories it was rolling up, suffragists from the larger, conservative organization put the change of atmosphere down to their own efforts.

All this is true, and yet the contribution of the Woman's Party to success should not be dismissed merely because it is difficult to measure. Picketing gave a feeling of urgency to the situation. It put the government in an untenable position. Miss Paul's followers were most respectable ladies, on occasion distinguished ones. What is a government to do when one of its prisoners is wearing a pearl necklace worth nine thousand dollars when being admitted to prison? It is embarrassing when senators appear in person to check on the situation of well-known prisoners. Besides, their treatment aroused protest throughout the nation. A situation such as had arisen could not continue, particularly during a war. Politicians in general were soon convinced of two things. They would not yield a foot to the outrageous Woman's Party, and yet something had to be done about suffrage at once. Its patient, suave, conservative tactics soon put the National-American in a position to profit from these feelings. Politicians felt no loss of face in giving in to them. The result was that Woman's Party pressure did seem to produce a change. Miss Paul's adherents freely claimed all the credit, while the other suffragists denied them any. The truth seems to have been that the major part of progress was due to the larger group, once it got started. Notwithstanding, Miss Paul's early work and the publicity earned by her pickets played a valuable part alongside the campaign of Carrie Catt.

The vote was set for January 10, 1918. A careful canvass of the opinions of House members had convinced the suffrage leaders on January first that they were forty-five votes short of the two-thirds majority they needed. True, forty-seven members were still doubtful; but was it likely they would all come down on the same side of the fence? A defeat would set back the suffrage cause possibly for years. Every effort was made to bring pressure on the doubtfuls. Prominent Republicans and Democrats were induced to declare for the amendment. Southern women were urged to telegraph their representatives, some of whom contended southern women did not want the vote. When one man went home, the suffrage state congressional chairman traveled back with him to the state line, while groups of suffragists were waiting at every station on his route. Influential women poured into Washington for last-minute interviews with their representatives.

Every effort was made by the suffrage organization to see that its supporters were marshaled to the last man for the great debate. But when the morning of the tenth dawned, there were long faces. Mr. Ireland of Illinois was held up by a train wreck. An Illinois suffragist had got an engine sent up the track with a messenger in it to get Mr. Ireland to sign a telegram authorizing the House to pair him off with an absent member of the opposition. It was doubtful whether his consent would appear in time for this procedure. Mr. Mann, also of Illinois, was in a hospital in Baltimore and had made no request to be paired. Mr. Barnhart of Indiana had been taken to a hospital in Washington. Mr. Crosser of Ohio was ill in bed. The wife of Mr. Hicks of New York had died last night. Mr. Sims of Tennessee had slipped on ice and broken his shoulder.. He had refused to have it set lest the anesthetic make it impossible for him to be in the House. He was actually present, but in such terrible pain that nobody knew how long he would be able to stay. In such circumstances, the momentous debate opened in the House.

For the women who crowded the galleries, weary hours followed. They had heard all the arguments on both sides and knew all the speakers. Authorization arrived from Mr. Ireland to pair his vote, but at the last minute no opponent could be found. The roll began.

Mr. Crosser had risen from his bed. Mr. Hicks had deserted the body of his dead wife in New York. Mr. Mann, who had been six months in the hospital, found strength to appear. Mr. Sims, his arm in a sling, not only voted but stayed on the floor to plead with his southern fellow members. Other supporters scoured anterooms to make sure all votes were counted.

As the second call started, Mr. Barnhart was brought in on a stretcher to vote his "Yea." The third call, aimed at those around the Speaker's desk who contended that they had not heard or made themselves heard, was itself inaudible to the watchers in the galleries. All was in doubt. The suffragists thought they had won, but Mr. Dominick of South Carolina demanded to vote "No" on the grounds that his name had not been called in the second roll. Uproar arose as members challenged this statement. Pounding for order, the Speaker made himself heard in Dominick's favor.

The opposition burst into applause as though they had won, but at the last moment a representative appeared to claim that he had voted on the first call, but that his "Yea" had not been recorded.

It was the suffrage turn to applaud; but before the totals

could be announced, the opposition demanded a recount. Solemnly the roll was called again, resulting in no changes. The suffrage amendment had passed the House with a majority of two-thirds plus two. If one man had changed over and one man not been present, it would have had to be done again from the beginning. How close the matter was could be seen when it was discovered that one representative, hopelessly undecided, had told his brother that if the child he was expecting turned out to be a girl, he would vote suffrage. It did, and he was recorded for the amendment.

Quite suddenly everyone was singing. A woman waiting outside the gallery for news had started "Praise God from Whom All Blessings Flow." The tune was taken up by hundreds waiting in the marble corridors. The suffrage amendment had passed the House. To be sure, it still had to pass the Senate and be ratified by the states, but in the excitement of the moment these seemed minor hurdles. The amendment had passed the House!

10

Winning the Senate
1918–1919

℧

Carrie Catt was jubilant. At last the long struggle neared its end. She even bought herself a new dress to wear when she started a round of states to campaign for ratification. In the meantime, she directed a letter to her state congressional chairmen, demanding a spate of telegrams, letters, and appeals to senators. Politicians have a natural tendency to get on the bandwagon, and Mrs. Catt felt confident that senators would be found in increasing numbers to vote for the amendment.

Mrs. Park, her lieutenant in Washington, was not so sure. Senators with their six-year term are not as susceptible as representatives to changes in popular demand. Besides, the Senate was the stronghold of the South, always averse to a constitutional amendment and especially to one whose wording bore a suspicious resemblance to the hated Fifteenth. A poll of senatorial opinion taken immediately after the House victory indicated fifty-four in favor. This was ten short of a two-thirds majority. There was nothing to be done but try for ten extra votes.

By April, eight votes had been acquired, by the filling of vacancies caused by death and by various pressures on individuals. Both Democratic and Republican National Committees had come out strongly for suffrage. Theodore Roosevelt and several Cabinet members had not only published letters favoring the amendment, but had also used their personal influence on their friends. Texas, Rhode Island, and North Dakota had given presidential suffrage to women, inducing three of their senators who were personally opposed to changing their vote. Activity in Washington had been frantic. Senator Jones of New Mexico, in charge of the Suffrage Committee, stood ready to bring up the bill at any moment. But until two more votes had been secured, there was no point in doing so.

Various political maneuvers followed. It seemed possible at first that the opposition, resigned to the inevitable, would let the bill go through by some arrangement. Absent members, for instance, might refrain from asking to be paired off against the bill's supporters. Twice in the spring and early summer Mr. Jones gave notice that he would bring up the bill. Each time, however, the opposition rallied, forcing him to withdraw rather than be defeated. When Congress recessed during the summer, nothing had been achieved.

Mrs. Catt, all the more disappointed because of her previous optimism, called for meetings of protest all over the country. Nonpolitical organizations such as the American Federation of Labor were persuaded to endorse the amendment. The President was induced to tack onto a letter to Mrs. Catt a sentence calling on the Senate to act. But the opposition was unaffected by any appeals.

September brought a fresh situation. The great influenza epidemic that raged throughout the world in 1918 produced a number of deaths in the Senate. Substitutes, appointed by governors for interim terms, were dark horses who had not faced an election campaign. There were in September two such unknowns, one a Republican, the other a Democrat. The Republicans implied that their man was in favor. The Democrats immediately set a day for the debate. It seemed most probable that one vote might be gained at the last minute from Democrats unwilling to bear the onus of rejecting the measure. But the Republicans either had spoken too soon or had intentionally led the Democrats into a trap. It was presently clear that they could not deliver the extra vote. In desperation Mrs. Catt turned to the President. Would he come down and appeal to the Senate in person?

President Wilson by now was a complete convert to the amendment. The war would soon come to an end, and Wilson's thoughts were on achieving a just peace. But Russia had pro-

"O SAVE US, SENATORS, FROM OURSELVES!"

Anti-suffrage forces presenting a petition to the Senate.
(*Culver Pictures*)

claimed votes for women. Germany was on the point of doing
so. England had promised woman suffrage after the war. Cana-
dians possessed it. The picketing of the Woman's Party had
made it awkward for Wilson to preach democracy abroad while
he struggled with suffrage at home. Besides, Miss Paul had lately
lost her patience. In August the Woman's Party had begun a
fresh series of demonstrations in Lafayette Square, opposite the
White House. Those taking part had been arrested for holding

meetings without a permit. Brought into court, they had declared that as a subject class without representation they did not come under the court's jurisdiction. They therefore refused to plead, give their names, or notice the proceedings in any way whatever. In fact, the whole dreary business of arrests, imprisonments, exposure of shocking conditions, and further demonstrations had started again. Nor was the versatility of Miss Paul in any way exhausted. Ten days before the Senate took up the amendment in September, President Wilson had said to a delegation of southern and western Democratic women:

"I am, as I think you know, heartily in sympathy with you. I have endeavored to assist you in every way in my power, and I shall continue to do so. I shall do all that I can to assist the passage of the Amendment by an early vote."

That very afternoon, the Woman's Party held a demonstration in Lafayette Square at which they publicly burned the President's words, declaring them hollow and empty. If he

Suffrage parade in Washington. (*Brown Brothers*)

really wanted to induce the Democratic senators to pass the measure, he could do so.

This was not the President's view of his own powers. All the same, the new demonstrations added to the difficulties of his position abroad. He was bound to deny that they affected his actions. Perhaps they did not, for he was already anxious about the measure. But they made it convenient to consent to Mrs. Catt's urging. He told the Senate that the amendment was necessary both for the prosecution of the war and for the attainment of a just peace. His interference with the processes of legislation, however, did no good. In fact, it gave offense. Nearly all the Democrats in opposition were southerners whose loyalty to the nominal leader of their party was far less intense than their devotion to the Old South. They feared that the enfranchisement of Negro women would spark a movement to apply the penal clauses of the Fourteenth Amendment against the South for denying Negroes the franchise. The appeal of the President made not a particle of difference. The motion was

defeated by the same two-vote margin that had twice earlier postponed it.

All was not yet lost, for a motion to reconsider was immediately made by the bill's supporters. The measure was placed once more on the Senate calendar. All the same, its defeat had encouraged its opponents; and there seemed no likelihood of breaking the deadlock.

Less than a week after the defeat of the amendment, pickets of the Woman's Party appeared in front of the Senate. They were promptly arrested by the Capitol police, who detained their banners but released the women themselves in fifteen minutes. That same afternoon they were back. A sort of game developed, watched by an interested public which now and then took part. Suffragists attempted to carry their banners up the Capitol steps. Police pounced on them, wrestled with them for the banners, twisted their wrists or pulled them to the ground. Presently they were taken to the guardroom, where they were released. They appeared again with a fresh set of banners. Inevitably tempers wore thin, and the police became gradually rougher. Some of the crowd, incensed against the pickets, also took a hand. Headlines again appeared throughout the nation. But where so many kinds of pressure had failed to produce two votes, it was not likely that a few pickets would be able to do so. Miss Paul, a realist, could hardly have expected so easy an answer.

Mrs. Catt was also ready for drastic measures. The November elections were coming up, and it was time the women took a hand. Being carefully nonpartisan, they picked two senators, one from each party, who were opposed to suffrage and standing against men thought to be in favor of it. Mrs. Catt decided to make a determined effort to unseat both. Accordingly, Senator Weeks of Massachusetts was handed over to the tender mercies of a woman's committee which got out a leaflet giving the senator's reactionary vote on thirteen measures in the last Congress. Page references were given in the *Congressional Record* in proof of the statements. This devastating pamphlet was sent to all registered Republicans and Progressives in the state, as well as to thirty-five thousand suffrage women, who were asked to obtain one vote each against him. A signed guarantee of the accuracy of the charges was obtained from the editor of the *Searchlight on Congress*. When Senator Weeks attempted to deny some of them, this was printed in the newspapers throughout the state just before the election.

Senator Weeks fell a victim to these tactics. Senator Saulsbury of Delaware was not so effectively attacked, since his opponent proved unwilling to give a pledge to vote for suffrage until two weeks before the election. However, a whirlwind campaign by the suffrage forces may well have tipped the balance. Senator Saulsbury was also defeated, though by a small margin.

The last session of the Sixty-fifth Congress opened with the assurance that the Sixty-sixth had a majority for the amendment. But in view of the 1920 presidential elections, it was not advisable to wait till the new Congress opened in May. There was a short session of the Sixty-fifth still to come; and it was arguable that the Democrats, perceiving that the new Senate with its Republican majority would pass the measure, might prefer to have the glory of passing it first. Moreover, the electors of South Carolina had rejected the senator appointed by their governor to fill a vacancy, electing for the short session a strong supporter of the suffrage amendment. One of the two missing votes was thus secured.

Every effort was made to find the other. Mass meetings were held all over the country. Letters poured in on congressmen by the thousand. Everybody was aware that only one vote held up the amendment. Indeed, Mrs. Park, still marshaling suffrage forces in Washington, had an amusing story to tell about a young thing from New York who came gaily into Suffrage House to see her.

"I came," the young lady said, "because they say you are a successful lobbyist, and I thought I'd like to be with you when you crack some tough old nut of a senator to get that last vote."

"Young lady," replied Mrs. Park in righteous wrath, "sixty-three senators, both national party committees, Cabinet members, and the President of the United States have thus far been unable to get that one vote. If I knew how to do it, do you suppose I would have waited for you to go with me?"

President Wilson, on the point of sailing for Europe, made another demand for suffrage before the joint session of Congress. Democratic women appealed to their party, pointing out that the result of the 1920 presidential election might well be determined by its action now. If the present Congress held up the suffrage amendment, the Republicans, in majority in the next Congress, would gain the glory. Nor could southern senators any longer appeal to their conviction on states' rights, since many of them had recently voted for the prohibition amendment.

One vote was still apparently lacking. President Wilson, keeping in touch from abroad, was more than ever insistent with his friends that the time had come to pass the suffrage amendment. Senator Williams was thought to be giving way. There was nothing to lose by putting the matter to the test, since time was running out for the Sixty-fifth Congress.

Meanwhile, however, the Woman's Party had once more taken a hand. Alice Paul was still convinced that the key to the whole matter was in the President's possession. That he was now anxious for the amendment she did not deny, but she did not consider that the issue took first place in his thoughts. She was unquestionably right. President Wilson was exerting himself to insure freedom among nations and the future peace of the world after the great conflict. It was hardly reasonable to expect that suffrage appeared of equal importance in his mind. To Miss Paul, however, it was. Political freedom was just as necessary in the United States as it was in Europe. If President Wilson would put all other matters aside and insist on the suffrage amendment, she was sure that he could obtain it from a Democratic Congress.

On January 1, 1919, the Woman's Party set up an urn filled with logs on the pavement outside the White House grounds directly opposite the front door. They solemnly lighted it. Alice Paul had decided to burn a "watchfire of freedom" there until the amendment was passed and to burn in it samples from the President's noble speeches in Europe as they were delivered. During such ceremonies a bell, installed above the door of Party headquarters, should toll to attract the attention of the public. This too very shortly became a sensational game. Police scattered the logs, which had been previously treated so that they were hard to put out. They brought up chemical extinguishers. While they were using them, surprise fires flared from the bronze urn in Lafayette Square. Later they popped up all over the little park. More arrests, more sentences, more hunger strikes took place. The women were prevented from maintaining a perpetual flame as they had intended, but nothing could stop them from assembling to burn the President's words on frequent occasions.

The vote on the suffrage amendment was set for February tenth. On February ninth, a Sunday, the bell over the Woman's Party headquarters tolled again. A hundred women emerged in a long procession bearing banners, wood, and an urn which they deposited in its usual spot opposite the White House door. This time they intended to burn the President himself in effigy, and there seems some doubt as to whether they actually succeeded. They certainly had with them a paper caricature which one of them is said to have dropped into the flames. But the police, outraged at this direct insult to the Head of State, were active at making arrests and breaking up the assembly. When the suffrage debate opened, the senators were also seething. Senator Williams insisted that he would never vote for a cause advocated by such methods. Perhaps this was only an excuse for voting as he had wished all along. In any case, the suffrage amendment failed of passing by one vote. It would have to pass the House again in the new Congress.

The Sixty-sixth Congress was called in special session by the President in May 1919, and the suffrage amendment passed through the House in less than a week. Not only had the elec-

tions brought new strength there, but all the tendencies of the
times were favoring the suffrage vote. The House resented being
held up by the Senate. Many representatives rushed to vote
with the winning side. The figures were three hundred four to
ninety, a startling contrast to the narrow majority of the preceding session, when a man had been carried in on a stretcher
to vote for the bill.

The amendment went to the Senate once more, and here at
long last the conclusion was foregone. There were sixty-six in
favor, two more than needed. There being therefore no reason
for delay, the suffrage amendment was brought up in three
weeks, passionately attacked in bitter oratory, eagerly defended,
and passed by the exact number of votes everyone had counted
beforehand.

It was seventy-one years since Elizabeth Stanton's original
meeting in Seneca Falls. Women had conducted fifty-six referenda campaigns, four hundred eighty campaigns to get state
legislatures to submit suffrage amendments to voters, forty-
seven campaigns to get state constitutional conventions to write
women suffrage into state constitutions, two hundred seventy-
seven campaigns to induce state party conventions to include
woman suffrage into state constitutions, two hundred seventy-
conventions to do likewise, and campaigns—some nominal but
some intensive—in nineteen successive Congresses.

Now at last, after all this turbulence and drama, the passing
of the Anthony Amendment was a cut-and-dried bit of business.
Hard work and persistence had conquered the country, and the
consent of the Senate seemed almost routine. Mrs. Catt was not
even watching from the gallery. She had attended the Senate
fiasco the preceding September and had suffered so bitterly that
she had determined never to do so again. A group of women
was present at the movie scene which recorded the signing, but
neither Carrie Catt nor Anna Shaw was among them. Alice Paul
had already left Washington to lobby the state legislatures in
session for ratification. The signatures of thirty-six states were
going to be needed.

11
Winning the Country
1919-1920

The last great battle of the suffrage movement was fought, surprisingly, in Tennessee. Nashua is a pleasant southern town of no great size. In August 1920 its chief hotel, the Hermitage, was bursting with forces gathered from all over the nation for a showdown. The Woman's Party was there, of course, with an office in Nashville and several full-time workers through the state. Alice Paul in Washington was pulling strings among politicians who might have influence on Tennessee. Carrie Catt, who had intended to leave the Tennessee workers in charge of Nashville, came down for a week in early July to smooth things out and found an emergency which kept her there two months. Meanwhile, red roses, worn by "Anti" women, clashed with the suffrage yellow in the Hermitage lobby. Mysterious men with brief cases represented railroad interests which, it was whispered, had long dominated Tennessee politics. These could be seen in conference with members of a manufacturers' lobby and with veterans of campaigns in many states against prohibition.

Tennessee was a dry state and had been so for some time. It had, moreover, already ratified prohibition. But as the legislators assembled in town for the special session that was to reject or confirm the suffrage amendment, they drifted into the elevators of The Hermitage and vanished in the direction of the eighth floor. A whisper seemed to go around, spread industriously by the businessmen circulating in the lobby. Friends and foes of suffrage alike slipped away for an hour or so, reappearing suspiciously red-faced and jolly. Could it be that the legislature was getting drunk? Pretty soon there could be no doubt about it. Horrified suffragists took counsel with such of their local friends as were coherent. Who knew what pledges might be given by a man in such a condition? That eighth-floor bar was blatantly illegal. It ought to be closed.

Possibly, but interference would be resented. "This is the Tennessee way."

"Are none sober?"

"Possibly." It began to be evident that this was a campaign with no holds barred.

The battle for ratification had been more hectic than it would have been if the Senate had passed the amendment early in 1918. The imminence of the 1920 elections, in which everyone wanted to vote, lent it urgency. Yet ratification must come through state legislatures, thirty of which were not to be in regular session. Mrs. Catt in her characteristic way had wasted no second. The amendment had passed the Senate on the fourth of June 1919. On that very same day telegrams went out from suffrage head-quarters to governors, calling for special sessions where they were needed. The signal was given to state organizations stand-ing ready to start a press campaign, to canvass legislators, or send deputations to governors. The last campaign of the woman suffrage movement swung straight into high gear.

The Illinois and Wisconsin legislatures were in session, but on the point of adjournment. The news was wired to them at once, and a race followed to see which could be the first to ratify. Illinois passed the amendment first, but Wisconsin was first to record its action in Washington. In the hurry, the Illinois resolution included a spelling error which was thought at first to invalidate it. The courts upheld it, however, though the leg-islature passed the motion again to make sure.

This promptness on the part of two states was no indication that ratification by thirty-four more would be easy to obtain. The liquor interests, opposing both suffrage and prohibition, threatened to demand referenda in eighteen or twenty states which had ratified but whose constitutions allowed for this proceeding. Since the methods of the liquor group in referenda campaigns were now notorious, it was understood that they might in this way defeat suffrage. The question was taken to the Supreme Court, which gave a decision banning referenda on a constitutional amendment. This decision, however, was not handed down till June 1920, only a few months before the coming election.

Even when this threat had been averted, the suffrage forces found it hard to win thirty-six states. Nine southern states had rejected the amendment or seemed certain to do so. This left only thirty-nine for the suffrage forces to work on. In June 1920 they had gained thirty-five, but had been looking for a last ratification since March.

The women had been anxious to roll up ratifications with speed, lest the impetus which had carried the measure through the Senate be lost. But the eagerness of the states was not so great. Special sessions were unpopular because of their expense. Thus even in favorable situations, great efforts were needed. The women spared themselves nothing, and ratifications mounted. But friends made haste while foes held back. The uncommitted states contained ever fewer friends of suffrage.

Connecticut and Vermont had seemed the best prospects. Both legislatures were thought to be in favor, but both governors were opposed. Vermont legislators even offered to pay their own expenses in special session, but nothing would induce their governor to call them together. The Connecticut governor challenged suffrage forces to prove an emergency justifying a session. A corps of forty-eight distinguished women, one from each state, assembled at Hartford and held a mass meeting there. Then they split up into teams, visiting every town, large or small. Eventually they came to the governor with resolutions from throughout the state asking for the special session. Hundreds of letters were sent in by prominent Republicans from all over the country. National Republican Headquarters added its pressure. Senator Warren Harding, soon to be Republican presidential candidate, sent an appeal. The governor, possibly hoping for a change in sentiment after the elections, steadily refused.

Balked in Vermont and Connecticut, the suffrage forces

pinned their hopes on Delaware, a strongly Republican state which was expected to ratify the amendment passed by a Republican Congress. Delaware, however, was split by political feuds. Opponents of suffrage played cleverly on internal jealousies. Delaware, by a narrow margin, rejected the amendment.

Attention was turned, perforce, to Tennessee, whose constitution forbade a ratification except in a regular session. But the Justice Department interpreted the late pronouncement of the Supreme Court to mean that a legislature might ratify the amendment any time it was called together. Governor Roberts was under pressure from President Wilson and was personally anxious to have the credit of passing the amendment. Two-thirds of Tennessee was southern and strictly Democratic, but there were feuds within the party. Roberts, who was due to stand for re-election, needed every advantage he could get. He consented therefore to call an emergency session. Meanwhile, the enemies of the measure contended that a local legislator was bound by his oath to the Tennessee constitution and must abide by its provisions, even if they proved illegal.

The legislature on which the attention of the country was now fixed had been intensively canvassed. Every member had been visited by deputations of women. At suffrage headquarters at Nashville reports had already been collected on each man's attitude, his friendships, relationships, or business connections with one side or the other. In particular he was rated bribable or not bribable. The suffrage forces thought it wiser not to count a bribable man as a supporter. Everyone so marked, as it turned out, voted against the amendment.

Influences of a sinister sort were felt from the first. Seth Walker, Speaker of the House, had pledged his vote to suffrage in writing. This did not prevent him from announcing a change of mind when the legislature met and becoming floor leader of the group opposing the motion. On August twelfth, the first day of committee hearings, the owner of the Nashville *Banner*, who had also promised support, spoke for the "Antis." Notwithstanding, the measure was favorably reported by the Senate committee and on the following day was passed by the Senate. Unwilling to attempt too much, the "Antis" concentrated on the House.

Here the vote was put off for about a week by delaying tactics while pressure was brought to bear on everybody who had signed a pledge to vote for the amendment. Members were offered political plums. They were threatened with business boycotts. They were entertained with whisky. Mysterious messages summoned them home. There was a rumor of a kidnaping attempt which actually did not, in the atmosphere of the Hermitage, appear incredible. The heat was dreadful, and whispering went on in every corner.

On the eighteenth of August the "Antis" felt strong enough to bring up a vote to table the measure and lay it aside without a debate. There were ninety-six representatives present out of ninety-nine. One place was vacant, and two friends of suffrage were ill. Of those present, one suffrage man had got up from bed after an operation and one had rushed back from California. But the "Antis" expected to count forty-nine against forty-seven.

The roll was called, and Representative Banks Turner, carried on the suffrage rolls as an "Anti," voted on the amendment side. Great was the sensation among friends and foes alike. Speaker Walker threw his arm around Turner and stood beside him while the roll was called again, beseeching him to change his vote. But Turner stood firm and, amid wild cheering, the motion to table was stalled forty-eight to forty-eight.

The suffrage supporters immediately moved for ratification. Harry Burn, the youngest of the representatives, was a newcomer only twenty-four years old. His rural district was against the amendment, and he had followed the wishes of his electors. Recently, however, his mother had sent him a letter imploring him in the strongest terms to vote for suffrage. Harry Burn had made up his mind that if the measure required a single extra vote, he would give it. He did so, and the count stood forty-nine to forty-seven for the amendment.

Speaker Walker immediately changed his vote to yes, for the

The State Senate in Tennessee votes to ratify the suffrage amendment, Nashville, Tennessee, 1920. (*Brown Brothers*)

purpose of a well-worn parliamentary maneuver. If he voted on the majority side, he could bring up a motion to reconsider the issue at any time within three days. In changing sides, however, he inadvertently deprived his supporters of a chance to challenge the ratification later. Fifty affirmative votes was a majority, not merely of the quorum present, but of the whole legislature. If not repealed after reconsideration, the ratification must stand.

There followed three days of fiercely intensified pressure to gain a vote or two for the "Antis." One representative was called up every half hour for two whole nights, each time with a different appeal to change his vote. Another was similarly urged all one night to go downtown and see a mysterious man of great importance. Harry Burn was threatened with an exposure of bribetaking. His mother was visited to try to induce her to deny her letter. Efforts to get representatives out of town were redoubled. Suffrage women picketed the hotel floors and counted their men every two hours all day long. Guards watched them all night. Even so, on the twentieth, when a vote was expected, one representative who had heard his baby was dying was actually on the train for home when a suffragist, driving to the station, promised him a special train if he would come back for that day's session.

The motion to reconsider was not brought up by Walker because the "Antis" lacked votes to defeat ratification. On the twenty-first of August it was possible for anyone else to introduce it. The suffrage forces intended to do so themselves and vote it down. But when they assembled, there was no quorum. Thirty-eight of the "Antis" had deserted in a body across the border into Alabama with the object of preventing reconsideration. The ratification forces went ahead without them. The governor was then enjoined by the "Antis" from notifying Washington. Such a restriction on his powers was an illegal one, and he disregarded it. On the twenty-sixth of August, the Secretary of State signed the suffrage amendment.

But the farce in Tennessee was not yet over. The "Antis," reappearing in a body after most of the legislature had gone home, voted to suspend the ratification. True, their position was considered illegal, but it was awkward. It did not look well to have the existence of the amendment hinge on a dispute. It seemed necessary to have the ratification of another state, which would put the issue beyond a doubt. Great pressure was therefore applied to the Connecticut governor to call the special session which he had long refused. That there was an emergency of sorts he could hardly deny, and he yielded at last. The Connecticut legislature ratified without delay. Once more, after all the shouting and the intrigue, the provision of an undisputed final vote was mere routine. The agitation in Tennessee died suddenly away. The amendment had become law, no matter what Tennessee said.

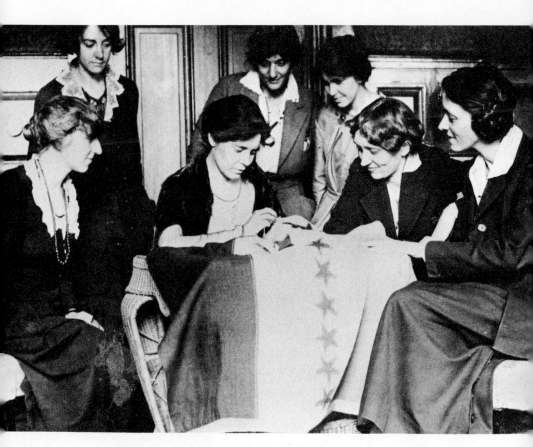

Alice Paul sewing the thirty-sixth star on the suffrage banner
to represent ratification by Tennessee, the thirty-sixth state.
(*Wide World Photos*)

The great struggle was over. The woman's movement
founded by Elizabeth Stanton had changed the climate of public opinion, the provisions of many laws, the opportunities open
to women. But ever since the Civil War, its concentration had
been on winning them the right to vote. For this women had
saved their pennies, spent their efforts, built up a tremendous
organization, learned how to run a political machine. By working for a single aim, they had gained the strength to win.
Women, however, would not go quietly home to domestic
duties. That could not be expected.

12

The Gains of Suffrage
1920-

What was really gained by the suffrage movement? After those nine hundred nine campaigns, those thousands of speeches, those trainloads of tracts, after the lifework of so many able women and the spare-time work of so many more, what was gained? When the parades and the pickets and the jail sentences were over, when Susan Anthony, Elizabeth Stanton, and Lucy Stone were dead, what good had they done? It is an interesting question.

One thing is certainly clear. The women who won the franchise in 1920 were different in outlook from the lady schoolteachers who had been scandalized when Susan Anthony got up to speak in 1853. They were even different from Lucretia Mott, gently fearing lest a demand for the vote make women ridiculous. How they had changed we may easily see by contrasting the Ph.D. of Alice Paul with the educational background of Susan Anthony. Remembering the sensation caused by the Bloomer costume, we may look at pictures of the bobbed hair, short skirts, and cigarettes of the twenties with a new understanding. A revolution had taken place.

Not all of the changes were the result of suffrage agitation. War, for instance, breaks down conventions. During the life of the suffrage movement, the United States went through two mighty wars. Other forces also were at work. The education of women was largely transformed by people who gave their lives to this one cause. Although generally friendly to suffrage, they were too much involved in education to give suffrage their time. The Temperance movement, which put through the prohibition amendment shortly before women gained the vote, got many to take part in community life, as did the women's clubs which spread over the nation after the Civil War. The entry of women into the professions was enormously assisted by the pioneer work of Clara Barton, Jane Addams, and others, who established new professions in nursing and social work. All of these advances were taking place at the same time that the work of the suffrage movement was progressing. One may even say that woman's new opportunities were a natural development of an industrial civilization, that they would have come even if women had stopped short of demanding the vote. They might have been slower in growth, but they would have appeared notwithstanding.

It would not be fair, however, to argue that the movement did nothing, simply because the changes it brought about were called for by the times. From its earliest beginnings, the woman's movement was a legal and political force. The Bloomer costume, the lady lecturers, the attacks of Elizabeth Stanton on the churches are minor things compared to the persistent pressure of the movement on legislatures and public opinion to improve woman's position in the eyes of the law. It is almost entirely because of these efforts that by 1920 in most states married women owned their own clothes, disposed of their own inheritance and earnings, were considered fit guardians for their own children, could sue, make contracts, and sign a will without their husbands' consent. Widows and unmarried women had likewise benefited and could look forward to a more dignified and independent life than in the past.

In this sense the good done for women by the movement was inestimable. Nineteenth-century history is full of shocking cases in which the defenselessness of women was exploited by their husbands, by their employers, or by the provision of the law. Besides, a life of dependence is too often deadly dull. The enrichment of so many uneventful lives was in itself of tremendous value. The woman's movement, though not the only force at work, served as a focus for all activities on woman's behalf. It played its own part in raising educational standards, destroying prejudice, training women to take some interest in public life. Elizabeth Stanton, lecturing on "Our Girls" from coast to coast, was broadcasting a picture of how girls ought to be brought up that looks surprisingly modern even today. Lucy Stone protesting against the conventional view of marriage and Susan Anthony asserting her right to sit on committees were giving examples which affected the public mind. The woman's movement cannot be isolated from other efforts to improve the lot of women. It partook of them all.

By 1920 so much had been achieved that it might appear the vote was hardly needed. Women's education was beginning to be comparable to men's. States that had lagged behind others were beginning to amend their laws. Complete equality of the sexes insofar as it could be achieved by law seemed only a question of time. Yet it is notable that the more of the new freedom women enjoyed, the more passionately they demanded the vote. The less they had to gain from it personally, the more they desired it.

Some of their feeling was undoubtedly due to the humiliation of being voteless. This country was founded on the principle that taxation without representation is an intolerable wrong. Now that the laws permitted it, many more women were property owners and had views on the subject of local tax assessments. Nor was it tolerable to educated women that immigrants who hardly knew the language should be hustled into the polling booths from which they were excluded. That great Irish humorist Mr. Dooley gives a picture of the situation which speaks for itself. The vote, says Mr. Dooley, "is men's wurruk. . . . It's meant f'r gr-reat sturdy American pathrites like Mulkowsky th' Pollacky down th' street. He don't know yet that he ain't votin' f'r th' King iv Poland. He thinks he's still over there pretendin' to be a horse instead iv a free American givin' an imytation iv a steam dhredge.

"On th' first Choosday afther th' first Monday in November an' April a man goes arround to his house, wakes him up, leads him down th' sthreet, an' votes him th' way ye'd wather a horse."

All this, however, was only half the reason why women in 1920 demanded the vote. They might have little to gain, but they had much they wanted to do. Excluded from political life and from the best positions in business or the professions, able women had made their mark in less commercial fields such as nursing, education, or social work. They had, in fact, taken up causes; and many had reforms which they desired to put through. Julia Lathrop and Grace Abbot of the Children's Bureau worked for laws protecting children. Florence Kelley, head of the Consumers' League, was interested in problems of merchandising. Dr. Alice Hamilton, pioneer worker in the field of industrial diseases, favored a host of measures regulating working conditions and establishing workmen's compensation. There were many other such leaders. Even less able women, brought up on Temperance agitation, were well aware of the vote's importance in local issues. In fact, some suffrage women were almost too apt to paint rosy pictures of the influence of women on political life. Social reforms would flourish. Political corruption, even war, would be no more. On the other side, businessmen concluded that hordes of women, full of self-righteous innocence, would rush to the polls and put through impractical measures destructive of business and prosperity.

These exaggerated hopes and fears proved unfounded. Social reforms have taken place, and women did help to introduce them. But the legislatures, congresses, and parties which have adopted them are still predominantly male. Political corruption is always with us, though it has changed its appearance since the dying of the saloon. The part that women have played in improvements is often hard to isolate, and the specific influence of the women's vote cannot be calculated. One thing we may unhesitatingly say: the votes of women have not put an end to the horrors of war.

Must we conclude that Susan Anthony was chasing a mirage? Women have now possessed the vote for more than forty-five years; and though the proportion who exercise it is steadily rising, it has never quite equaled the proportion of voting men. Our ancestors, some of them, fought harder for this privilege than for any other. But we are a later generation. Are we to be proud of what they achieved, or just indifferent? What became of all the enthusiasm and fire of the suffrage movement? The winning of New York took the intensive efforts of many thousand women for five years. What of Miss Paul, sitting up all night in F Street, the stenographers dropping in to help after work, the women shoppers haled off the street to get the letters out? What became of the political skills women had acquired, the knowledge of where to apply pressure to get things done? Surely these could not be dropped because the amendment was ratified by Tennessee. It would have been a tragedy if capable women all over the country had gone home to put up their feet.

Such actually had been Miss Paul's original intention. She had worked for the vote, and it was won. She was not personally ambitious. But the Woman's Party had swallowed the WSPU of Harriot Blatch, which in its turn had stressed trade-union connections. Having no contented conservative wing, the party was sensitive to pressure from women who still had grievances. These proved to be many. It was not merely that the southern states had lagged behind in granting women rights comparable to men's. It was rather that the whole body of law had been put together on the assumption that woman was an inferior creature. Bits and pieces remained embedded in every structure, even when the chief causes of complaint were removed. Married women, for instance, were entitled in New York State to own their own earnings, provided they had a paid job outside the home. This was small consolation for the wife who lived over her shop or ran a boardinghouse. Her drunken husband might claim whatever she earned. In several states where husband and wife entered business together, the man had entire control over his wife's share.

These and many other instances of legal unfairness might not press hard on many women, yet all of them affected some.

More insidious and more widespread were the troubles that beset all women who needed to earn a living. The majority of women were still confined to the lowest-paid trades, which were either unorganized or directed by an entirely male union leadership. Professional women saw advancement go to men, often younger and with less ability. It was especially with the economic problems of women in mind that the Woman's Party started out on a fresh crusade more complex than the first.

There was no longer a dramatic issue to arouse the mass of American women. The Woman's Party had always been more energetic than numerous, and its tactics had alienated the larger movement. In fact, it had made itself thoroughly disliked by numbers of either sex and must pay the penalty for its earlier successes. But Miss Paul and those who worked with her had courage and experience in political fights. Some new allies might be expected, especially from among professional women. The Woman's Party, on whom the mantle of Miss Anthony now seemed to fall, advanced to the fight.

Two years of agitating for reforms convinced Miss Paul that the task she had taken up was endless. To root out every piece of discrimination in every state might take a century. Meanwhile, laws protective of women in industry were being added to the statute book and were supported both by trade unions and many reformers. The result, in Miss Paul's view, was to depress the woman worker. To limit her hours does not give a woman protection. It throws her out of work. This has been clear to her competitors. A New York law forbidding waitresses to work after ten at night was enthusiastically supported by waiters, since the later the hour, the larger the tip. Hat-check girls and charwomen, who face no male competition, were allowed to work when they pleased without protection.

Thus forced to combat both the relics of the past and the trends of the present, the Woman's Party saw no answer save a federal amendment. Accordingly they drafted a new one which stated explicitly that "Equality of rights under the law shall not be denied or abridged by the United States or by any State on account of sex." This was christened the Lucretia Mott Amendment in honor of the most beloved of the early feminists. Introduced for the first time in 1923, it has by now gained a respectable body of opinion in both Senate and House, together with the support of some distinguished women's organizations in the country at large. Its critics, and they have been many, call it so sweeping as to be unenforceable. In particular, they point out that besides abolishing special laws for the protection of women in industry, it would make women liable to be drafted for war. Its supporters claim that both are necessary. In the armed forces women already have a place, and impartial treatment does not mean that all are qualified for identical jobs. In industry, the removal of discriminatory laws should start a reversal of tendencies which are still at work today. For instance, in 1961 the median wage of all women with one to four years of college was lower than that of colored men with one to four years of high school. Even admitting that many such women work for a few years, this presents a depressing picture.

Of one thing we may be sure. If the Lucretia Mott Amendment were ever to go through, a remarkable hodgepodge of old-fashioned laws would be repealed. It would become impossible to keep women from jury duty. Women everywhere would have equal rights with their husbands over their children, could seek divorce on identical grounds, and could not be the victims of discriminatory laws passed by state legislatures.

Such has been the battle of the Woman's Party. It has been additionally active in various measures which have come up at the national level. Notably it was instrumental in getting the citizenship laws so changed that women who marry foreigners now possess the same rights as do men who marry foreign women. It has also succeeded in getting the fair-employment section of the Civil Rights Act broadened to prohibit discrimination against women.

The Woman's Party today appeals mainly to professional women who have often been kept back by their sex from obtaining promotion. The party is small and works in alliance with other women's organizations. But it still has energy and still keeps watch on Washington. Headquarters are a handsome old brick house with a history, situated on Capitol Hill, convenient to Congress and the Supreme Court. Here the party displays a collection of mementos of the past, including busts and portraits of women leaders. Among them, Miss Paul is represented only by a poor likeness. The fact is typical. Miss Paul cares deeply for records of the past, but her attention is given to the present and the future.

Carrie Catt, who was nearing sixty when suffrage was won, was not personally ambitious either. She had taken the presidency of the Association with reluctance. She was now about to lay it down. Her reward had been the victory itself and one of those triumphal days which come occasionally to national figures. She had gone straight from Tennessee to Washington, where the Secretary of State had invited her over to see the proclamation he had just signed. She had made a great speech at a meeting that night, and on the next day had taken a train home to New York. At every stop deputations of women were waiting to greet her, their arms full of flowers. In New York, the governor was on hand at the station to tender his congratulations. The Woman Suffrage Party of New York formed a procession to conduct her to her hotel with the officers of the national association marching beside her automobile like a guard of honor. There we may leave her with flowers in her arms and her face alight with joy. She had already given thought to the future of the movement. It was not Carrie Catt's way to come up to a new situation unprepared.

In 1919, Mrs. Catt had proposed to the National-American that on the granting of the vote it transform itself into a League of Women Voters. The organization of this should be the old one. Local branches would be federated into state groups with a national board over all. The suffrage association should continue to exist, but for new purposes.

The first of these should be to help the woman voter. Naturally many women were inexperienced in political problems and lacking in confidence. The League should consider ways to make such women effective citizens. After all, suffrage had given its members vast experience in what really amounted to adult education on a political level. The League had the organization and the workers which had put suffrage across. Surely the spirit of Elizabeth Stanton, so eager to educate her own sex, need not die.

With such ideas in mind, the League of Women Voters soon plunged into a campaign to get women to vote. With the ingenuity which had always characterized the movement, it invented a number of techniques which were later taken up by political parties, such as volunteer baby-sitters, free transportation, and telephone squads. It set up citizenship schools and demonstrations on how to mark a ballot. It made a digest of the qualifications demanded by each state for voter registration and started a campaign to simplify these. Later it began to put out the election leaflets everyone finds so useful, telling who the candidates are, what their background is, and their position on current questions.

These and other such efforts induced an increasing number of women to vote, but never enough to satisfy the League. It presently dawned on workers that they must interest women in voting by showing them what effect they could have on the course of events. The League's educational program was broadened to include community study, through which a woman can see what needs doing locally on such things as zoning, schools, slum clearance, or public parks. It set women to work on useful projects which they could handle in their own communities. It taught them in this way what the political process in a democracy is, how things get done. As their vision widened, women were no longer victims of the frustration and inertia that plague the nonvoter. They understood better where to give their little push and set a ball rolling. Perhaps an account of one such community effort may serve as an example of countless others.

In 1958, the town of Burlington, Vermont, needed a sewage-disposal plant. The League of Women Voters, which had been concerning itself with the sewage problems of Burlington for over ten years, threw itself into the fight. The first necessary step was to get an enabling act through the state legislature so that the town might issue bonds exclusive of the limits set in its charter. Next the League began to go to work on public opinion. League members went up to the Health Department to get instruction on how to take water samples from Lake Champlain to test for contamination. They started to obtain them every week during the summer, using pretty girls to swim out for their samples and making certain that the local newspaper photographers knew when they were going. Other similar stunts kept the papers full of contamination news throughout two summers. Next came a big meeting, and the plan was put up to the city council.

Complications multiplied. An asphalt plant had to be removed from the only site available for the sewage plant. The League campaigned for an election to enable the town to do so. A petition was organized to rescind the vote because of the cost of the proposed plant. Another election campaign brought another vote—and another petition. The League then made a drive to inform each individual who had signed the last petition of the facts of the case. As a result, most of these withdrew their names. Soon another campaign had to be launched to support a bond issue. Doorbells were rung again. Posters and banners appeared. There were more water samples taken, more news stories, more telephoning. The whole process took three years, but the citizens of Burlington got their sewage plant. "Cost," says the League report, "in money to the League was $15.00." It would be interesting to know what it cost in terms of the time of League members.

Work of this kind lacks the glamor of the great suffrage parades and open-air meetings. But it has resulted in an immense number of local improvements, and it has trained many political workers. These have often gone on to what the League also had in mind, the putting through of measures worthwhile to the state or the nation at large. For if the Woman's Party has taken up most of the work directly for women, the League of Women Voters has fallen heir to the general reforming zeal of the suffrage movement. To those who think the value of the woman's vote depends not on the good women got from it, but on what they did with their political powers, the League of Women Voters seems truly important.

It would not be fair to say that the League, which is a comparatively small organization today, inherited all the reforming zeal of suffrage. Some women preferred a special cause. Others chose to work through political parties. But the League, like the suffrage movement, remained outside the political system. Deliberately nonpartisan, it uses suffrage techniques. The League of Women Voters of Massachusetts recently put through a campaign to restrict the powers of the Governor's Council, a relic of colonial times which had become an obstacle to decent government in the Commonwealth. The careful detailed instructions of the League to its amateur lobbyists exactly remind one of the tactics of Maud Park in Washington. Graft and patronage are particularly hard to reform by legislative action, and the measure was tied, a hundred and six to a hundred and six. But the League, whose political strength had astonished friend and foe alike, took the question to referendum and got it passed after a campaign which again drew largely on suffrage experience and methods.

To say that the League of Women Voters has taken over the old suffrage techniques is to pay it a compliment of a special kind. In the days when they were working for the vote, women had to bring pressure on the political world from the outside. In this respect, the position of the League today is unique among our political organizations. Men have nothing comparable to it. There are special interests at work in the lobbies of Congress and of state legislatures. These, however, have an axe to grind. The League supports a measure on its merits alone, seeking to focus the idealism of women for action. Not one cause, but a number of causes, selected in the organization by a democratic process, are given League support. More nearly therefore than any one other organization it provides the answer to the most important question of all—not "What did women get from the vote?" but "What have they done with it?"

They have done a good deal and in a great many fields. The League of Women Voters likes best to investigate subjects that have not yet caught public attention. A few years back, for instance, it began to study our use of our water resources. A picture that had not previously been clear to anyone emerged. For instance, twenty-five departments of the federal government were discovered to have jurisdiction, often conflicting, over our water resources. The League of Women Voters did much of the pioneer work necessary for the Water Resources and Planning Act of 1964. On the state and local level, flood and pollution control has been actively supported by League efforts. Its educational work has been developed by a series of regional conferences on the use of water basins which have drawn together all organizations interested in a special area.

The work of the League on our water resources is a typical example of League activity as a whole. It is obviously useful. It is nonpartisan. It requires a great deal of detailed study and has ramifications at every level of government. It attracts, as many of the League's causes do, the interest of other organizations. Thus if an important law is passed dealing with this subject, no one can precisely measure the League's contribution. The records of this lie locked in files of the League which nobody takes time to investigate. League citizens are pressing on to cope with the future.

There is nothing romantic or historic about the national headquarters of the League of Women Voters in Washington. It is not decorated with portraits of suffrage leaders. Its memories really begin with Maud Wood Park, who became its first president in 1920. The place is not a club where people can drop in to chat. It is a set of offices where practical women sift reports, send out literature, coordinate efforts, and make the

The Woman's Party displays a victory banner from the balcony of their national headquarters in Washington. Note the stars in the flag, one for each state that has granted woman suffrage. Such flags were displayed at parades and on all important suffrage occasions. (*The Bettmann Archive*)

necessary moves at a national level. Miss Anthony's little "desk with pigeonholes" would be lost in such a place. Yet the generous spirit of those early reformers is undoubtedly present. They too were active in many progressive movements.

It is natural enough that the League of Women Voters and

the Woman's Party between them contain only a small proportion of the women for whom the vote was won. Perhaps women who are politically active in conventional ways may also be counted among the heirs of the suffrage movement. They, however, are few in number. To the majority of women, the vote may often appear less a privilege than a challenge. The right—indeed the duty—to vote does not make life simpler for a busy woman. In a huge democracy it is hard to get good candidates or, having got them, to know which they are. It is often difficult to understand vital issues. Perhaps it is tempting to conclude that the twentieth century makes altogether too many demands, and that voting is just another of these. But if so, it is now an equal demand on men and women. Women have claimed education and opportunities comparable to men's. They can no longer leave men to solve the problems that both sexes face. Voting cannot be left to an arbitrary part of the population, no more intelligent, not necessarily wiser or more patriotic. Women must vote, not because they have an axe to grind, not because it is their whim, not because men do it. It is not even necessary that they make a special contribution as women. They must vote because it is no longer possible for government to rest on the consent of half the people.

Important Dates
in the Woman Suffrage Movement

ℰ

1848   Foundation of movement by Elizabeth Cady Stanton in Seneca Falls, New York.

1869   Split of movement into National Woman Suffrage Association led by Miss Anthony and Mrs. Stanton, and American Woman Suffrage Association, led by Mrs. Stone and her husband, Henry Blackwell.

1869   Territory of Wyoming adopts woman suffrage.

1872   Miss Anthony votes in Rochester, New York, and is prosecuted for voting illegally.

1889   The suffrage associations merge into the National-American Woman Suffrage Association.

1890   Wyoming admitted to the Union as a woman suffrage state.

1892   Death of Mrs. Stone. Retirement of Mrs. Stanton.

1893   Colorado won as a woman suffrage state.

1896   Idaho won as a woman suffrage state.

1896   Utah admitted to the Union as a woman suffrage state.

1900   Retirement of Miss Anthony.

1907   Woman's Political Union founded by Harriot Stanton Blatch; puts new life into the movement.

1909   Woman Suffrage Party, organized in New York by Carrie Catt, is the first attempt to win a great city by using political methods.

1910   Washington won as a woman suffrage state.

1911   California won as a woman suffrage state.

1912   Alice Paul arrives in Washington to work for the federal amendment. She soon founds the Congressional Union, later the Woman's Party.

1914   Illinois legislature grants women presidential suffrage.

1915   Mrs. Catt takes over the National-American and soon presents the winning plan.

1917   The Woman's Party pickets the White House.
1917   New York won as a woman suffrage state.
1918   The federal amendment passes the House.
1919   The federal amendment passes the Senate.
1920   The federal amendment is ratified by two-thirds of the states.

Suggestions
for Further Reading

❧

1. MODERN BIOGRAPHIES OF WOMAN LEADERS:
    Susan B. Anthony, Her Personal History and Her Era
    (Katharine Anthony; New York: Doubleday, 1954)
    Susan B. Anthony: Rebel, Crusader, Humanitarian
    (Alma Lutz; Boston: Beacon Press, 1959)
    Carrie Chapman Catt
    (Mary Gray Peck; New York: H. W. Wilson Co., 1954)
    Lucretia Mott
    (Otelia Cromwell; Cambridge, Mass.: Harvard University Press, 1958)
    Created Equal
    (Alma Lutz; New York: John Day, 1940)
    Biography of Elizabeth Cady Stanton
    Morning Star
    (Elinor Rice Hays; New York: Harcourt, Brace, 1961)
    Biography of Lucy Stone

2. INTERESTING BOOKS BY WOMAN LEADERS:
    Up Hill with Banners Flying
    (Inez H. Irwin; Penobscot, Me.: Traversty Press, 1964)
    Activities of the Woman's Party
    Lifting the Curtain
    (Caroline Katzenstein; Philadelphia: Dorrance, 1955)
    Activities of the Woman's Party
    Front Door Lobby
    (Maud Wood Park, edited by Edna L. Stantial; Boston: Beacon Press, 1960)
    Excellent account of work in the Washington lobby
    Woman Suffrage and Politics
    (Carrie C. Catt and Nettie R. Shuler; New York: Scribner, 1923)
    The secret opponents of woman suffrage

183

3. MODERN BOOKS ON THE WOMAN'S MOVEMENT IN GENERAL:

Century of Struggle
(Eleanor Flexner; Cambridge, Mass.: Harvard University Press, 1959)

The Better Half: The Emancipation of the American Woman
(Andrew Sinclair; New York: Harper & Row, 1965)

American Feminists
(Robert E. Riegel: Lawrence, Kan.: University of Kansas Press, 1963)

Index

Water Resources and Planning
Act (1964), 178
WCTU (Woman's National
Christian Temperance Un-
ion), 77-81
Weeks, Sen. John W., 154-55
White House, picketing of, 122-
33, 156-57
Williams, Sen. John S., 156, 157
Willard, Emma, 23
Willard, Frances Elizabeth, 74-81
Willard, Josiah, 74
Wilson, Woodrow, 115-17, 118-
19, 121-23, 125, 139-40, 150,
156-57
Wisconsin, women's suffrage in,
160
Woman Suffrage Party, 103-105
Woman's Journal (newspaper),
55-57
Woman's Loyal League, 49
Woman's National Christian
Temperance Union
(WCTU), 77-81
Woman's Party, 120-21, 146-47,
151-52, 159, 171-74
picketing of Senate by, 154
picketing of White House by,
122-33, 156-57

Woman's Rights Conventions, 41
in Seneca Falls, N.Y., 27-31
in Worchester, Mass., 34
Woman's State Temperance So-
ciety, 35
Convention (1852) of, 36-37
Woman's War, 76-77
Women's Anti-Slavery Associa-
tion, 26
Women's Political Union, 101-
102
Women's Social and Political
Union (WSPU), 98
Woodhull, Victoria, 57-60
Woodhull and Claflin's Weekly,
59, 60
Woodward, Charlotte, 30-31
Worcester, Mass., Woman's
Rights Convention, 34
World Temperance Convention
(1853), 37-38
World War I, 121, 124-25, 143
WSPU (Women's Social and Po-
litical Union), 98
Wyoming, women's suffrage in,
70-72

Younger, Miss, 114